CAD at Work

D1710555

The Visual Technology Series
Carl Machover, Series Advisor

BUEHRENS • *DataCAD for Architects and Designers,* 0-07-008914-0

HELLER/HELLER • *Multimedia Business Presentations,* 0-07-028080-0

HODGE • *Interactive Television: A Comprehensive Guide for Multimedia Technologists,* 0-07-029151-9

JOHNSON • *LabVIEW Graphical Programming,* 0-07-032692-2

KEYES • *The Ultimate Multimedia Handbook,* 0-07-034530-9

LARIJANI • *Virtual Reality Primer,* 0-07-036416-8

MACHOVER • *The CAD / CAM Handbook,* 0-07-039375-3

REYNOLDS/IWINSKI • *Multimedia Training: Developing Technology-Based Systems,* 0-07-912012-1

In order to receive additional information on these or any other McGraw-Hill titles, in the United States please call 1-800-822-8158. In other countries, contact your local McGraw-Hill representative. **KEY=WM16XXA**

CAD at Work

Making the Most of Computer-Aided Design

Ashley J. Hastings

McGraw-Hill

New York   San Francisco   Washington, D.C.   Auckland   Bogotá
Caracas   Lisbon   London   Madrid   Mexico City   Milan
Montreal   New Delhi   San Juan   Singapore
Sydney   Tokyo   Toronto

Library of Congress Cataloging-in-Publication Data

Hastings, Ashley J.
    CAD at work : making the most of computer-aided design / Ashley
J. Hastings.
        p.   cm.—(McGraw-Hill series on visual technology)
    Includes index.
    ISBN 0-07-027022-8 (pbk.)
    1. Design, Industrial—Data processing. 2. Computer-aided design.
I. Title. II. Series.
TS174.4.H37 1996   96-47202
620'.0042'0285—dc21   CIP

McGraw-Hill

*A Division of The **McGraw·Hill** Companies*

Copyright © 1997 by The McGraw-Hill Companies, Inc. All rights
reserved. Printed in the United States of America. Except as permitted
under the United States Copyright Act of 1976, no part of this
publication may be reproduced or distributed in any form or by any
means, or stored in a data base or retrieval system, without the prior
written permission of the publisher.

1 2 3 4 5 6 7 8 9 0 DOC/DOC 9 0 1 0 9 8 7 6

ISBN 0-07-027022-8

*The sponsoring editor of this book was Jennifer Holt DiGiovanna, the
editing supervisor was Fred Bernardi, and the production supervisor
was Donald F. Schmidt. It was set in New Century Schoolbook
by McGraw-Hill's Professional Book Group composition unit,
Hightstown, N.J.*

Printed and bound by R. R. Donnelley & Sons Company.

McGraw-Hill books are available at special quantity discounts to use as
premiums and sales promotions, or for use in corporate training
programs. For more information, please write to the Director of Special
Sales, McGraw-Hill, 11 West 19th Street, New York, NY 10011. Or
contact your local bookstore.

Information contained in this work has been obtained by The
McGraw-Hill Companies, Inc. ("McGraw-Hill") from sources
believed to be reliable. However, neither McGraw-Hill nor its
authors guarantee the accuracy or completeness of any information published herein and neither McGraw-Hill nor its
authors shall be responsible for any errors, omissions, or dam-
ages arising out of use of this information. This work is published with the understanding that McGraw-Hill and its
authors are supplying information but are not attempting to
render engineering or other professional services. If such services are required, the assistance of an appropriate professional should be sought.

 This book is printed on recycled, acid-free paper containing a
minimum of 50% recycled de-inked fiber.

To my wife and my parents
for their support and understanding.

Contents

Part 7   Project Planning

Part 8   Quality Assurance (QA)

Foreword

There is now broad acceptance in the role of CAD in improving corporate competitiveness. The return on investment from the purchase of a CAD system is well appreciated (more than 70% of UK engineering design companies have invested in CAD). However, many still see CAD as a point solution to replace a drawing board with a CAD system—but CAD offers much more than that.

The promise of CAD is to completely design, visualize, cost, and predict "in-service" behavior of a design before even making a prototype! To achieve that promise companies need to make CAD part of their design process and not simply a replacement for the drawing board. Fundamentally, it is much cheaper to make and correct our mistakes in a computer than on-site or in the final product.

The benefits are there to be realized, but achieving them demands a holistic view of the whole design methodology and the approach to investment in it. Achieving them means seeing the bigger picture and the bigger potential as opposed to the point solution of drawing production. People really need to quantify the management effects that CAD has on project control, quality, team skill, supplier relationships, training investment, and financial justification.

In summary, Ashley Hastings's work in compiling this book has produced an entertaining and practical guide to achieving a sophisticated return on investment from your CAD system.

Jeff Drust
MANAGING DIRECTOR, AUTODESK LTD.

Preface

Why should you read this book? Well, here's why I wrote it.

The Bad Old Days

I remember my Technical Drawing classes at school. I had all the equipment — compass, ruler, eraser, those flimsy plastic things with lots of different-sized circles cut out of them, one of those bendy sticks that could be molded into any curve, and a whole bundle of pencils. Initially I even had a slide rule, though these became obsolete before I had managed to figure out what to do with them.

In the early lessons, this fine selection of equipment was put to use drawing basic 3-dimensional solids. This seemed too easy. I had mastered the art of drawing rectangles, circles, and triangles at the age of two and had become equally proficient in building block work soon after that. This was going to be easy. However, I was being overly confident.

There were three problems. First, there were rules to learn about what view of the shape was to be drawn where: too high and the drawing crept off the sheet and onto another piece of paper hastily tacked on to catch the overspill; too far to one side and it encroached on the space allocated for the end elevation.

The second problem was the grime. Where did it all come from? I would sit at my drawing board scrubbed so clean I could have been about to perform open-heart surgery, and then after only a few minutes grubby fingermarks would appear on my paper. It would get worse— dark bands of grime would appear out of nowhere, making my drawing look as if someone had just trodden on it while I was not looking.

These two problems were compounded by a third: the constant battle raged between me and my drawing tools. A circle seemed simple enough to draw, but after I had put my compass into action, holes and scratches were everywhere, as if Freddy Kruger had been sitting at my drawing board. As if this were not bad enough, when it came to placing a neat centerline through the circle, the pencil would catch on the crater left behind by the compass, leave its sharp point behind, and careen away from the ruler's side and across the drawing.

So it was not as easy as I had anticipated.

The annoying thing was that, in my mind, I could do the work. I understood the theory perfectly well, and I could visualize complex solids from numerous viewpoints. The difficult bit was the actual method of putting it onto paper.

I managed to scrape through my Technical Drawing examination, but I left school feeling that no matter what great designs I conceived in my mind, they were likely to go no further. As it happens, I never did conceive of any great designs, but if I had, life would have been pretty frustrating.

Still, the thought of all the creative potential that must exist, yet never see the light of day because of an inadequate method of conveying the information, is something that has always stayed with me.

A Brave New World

One day I saw an advertisement in a local newspaper for a nine-week course in "Computer-aided Design and Manufacture" (CADCAM). This looked interesting. I enrolled, and it was. Here was a way of putting ideas onto paper without any of the obstacles that had previously gotten in my way.

The course was wide-ranging and did not dwell much on CAD other than to introduce us to the basics. That did not matter. I could tell immediately that CAD was a world where I could explore on my own; all that was needed was someone to show me the way in. The more I discovered, the more I wanted to know this world inside-out.

New rules seemed to apply. If I wanted to see a circle, centered at a specific point and tangential to another circle, it was there in an instant. The chores of calculation and presentation did not exist, and what is more, it was perfectly accurate — not the artistic approximations of before — and I could alter it as many times as I liked without peppering the paper with compass holes.

I had an advantage over many of my classmates. Many of them had trained and worked for many years on the drawing board. This meant that they brought with them a frame of mind that had no place in the CAD environment. Breaking free of this mental straight-jacket seemed more difficult than learning the CAD way of working, which was all I had to contend with.

Even toward the end of the course I recall a fellow student puzzling over his computer with a ruler pressed firmly onto the screen. To him, the screen was an electronic piece of paper. He had drawn a line 10cm long and he expected it to appear 10cm long. He just could not accept the concept of the computer screen as a window through which the subject is viewed, whatever its size — just like television. Yet, as far as I believe, he did not think everyone on television was only 15cm tall.

Where Did We Go Wrong?

I have never trained as a designer (not surprisingly, after the unpromising start I had in my Technical Drawing lessons), so after my CADCAM course I became an "operator," operating the CAD system for the benefit of others.

Manual designers were used to having an idea and then spending most of their time putting it onto paper. I could take the same idea and play with it. People would leave their drawing boards to watch me experiment with variations on a design, explore a range of "what if" scenarios and maneuver elements of drawings like a magician. They would look over my shoulder, astonished at the magic taking place.

It is true that at this time you could impress people by sitting at a computer and doing absolutely anything. Even the most basic CAD work had a futuristic glamor. However, its appeal was well founded and it soon became clear that this was the way to go for the design industry. CAD was not just another design tool but was a whole new way of working.

We have seen since the mid-1980s CAD skills become more and more commonplace. Now it is the manual designer that stands out from the crowd, like a blacksmith bending over his anvil and other quaint characters of yesteryear.

The route from drawing board to CAD became a well-trodden path. But these converts brought with them a lot of baggage. Unfortunately, it seems you can take the designer away from the drawing board but you can't take the drawing board away from the designer. That is, somewhere along the line CAD ceased being a new way of working and became little more than an electronic drawing board. To me, this was like watching someone buy a car and then tie two horses to the front to pull it along.

Then things took another step backwards. Design office procedures that had evolved over many years were abandoned when CAD came into the building. Where once projects would have followed a closely monitored plan, work would start on the CAD system with minimal intervention by the Project Manager. It was as if, because it involved computers, people expected it all to happen on its own.

There was little or no management strategy where CAD was concerned. Money was spent on technology without the careful planning that usually accompanies such a major investment. No one in the upper echelons of management had any idea of the potential of the system that they had spent so much money on.

Projects would get into a mess that would previously have been pre-empted and dealt with at an early stage. Valuable CAD data went unexploited as other departments preferred paper, as they had always done in the past.

When CAD designers were employed all that was requested were CAD skills — whatever the specific requirements of the project they were to be working on. The attitude seemed to be "the computer does all the work and the CAD user just prints it out when needed."

Design work suffered as technical problems dominated: bad connections, lost data, poor quality plots, computer faults, corrupt software, etc. Talented designers began to regard CAD as a dead-end, more a place for computer nerds than creative types.

Not surprisingly, the enthusiastic attitudes that greeted CAD's arrival soon began to wane.

Help!

This is a crazy way of working and a criminal waste of the CAD opportunity. At first I thought it was only me, but as a CAD Manager and later as a CAD Consultant, I realized that, though some companies were coping better than others, this is an industrywide problem.

What makes matters worse is that there is no help around. Bookshelves groan under the weight of material published on CAD, but it is all little more than a tutorial rehash of the technical manual provided with the software.

We have enough books to tell us what to type at the keyboard. What is needed is a book that tells us how to apply CAD effectively in the workplace.

Well, that's what I thought, and that's why this book was written. I hope you enjoy it.

Acknowledgments

Thanks to Autodesk Ltd., for providing the illustrations used in Figs. 3-1, 9-2, and 20-1. Thanks also to Martin Lewy for kindly lending me his computer when mine wasn't up to it.

Ashley J. Hastings

Introduction

Since computer technology first found its way into the design office, there have been no shortage of products, books, magazines, and companies vying for the computer-aided designer's attention. As the technology has developed and expanded throughout the business, so the supply of goods and services to support the growing need has continued to increase.

One would be forgiven for thinking that, thanks to this attention, a majority of the CAD users' needs were being addressed. Well, this has not been the case.

The attention has focused, almost entirely, on the "computer operating" aspect of CAD: Tutorials for the beginner, support for the user, advanced techniques for the specialists, products to buy, training to use them, technical support for when they break down.

Beyond the computer keyboard, however, is the real world of the workplace. Here, CAD is an investment that must reap rewards, skills have to relate to business needs, and new working methods must be functional. These practical consequences must be understood by anyone wishing to put CAD to effective use. Yet, the fact is, they are alarmingly neglected.

This book addresses this serious deficit by providing a comprehensive, jargon-free strategy for the effective application of CAD that will allow individuals and whole companies alike to seize its full potential.

This is the first book for today's design industry that tells the full story of how to make the most of CAD. It is written with the understanding that CAD is not simply a piece of equipment but a new way of working that warrants new approaches to management, staff, and workload.

The chapters that follow this introduction provide an exploration of these issues. Rather than bombarding the reader with a barrage of figures, the discussions of facts in this book are more philosophical than numerical. The result is an accessible treatise on the subject as well as an operational reference.

Why This Book Is Important

Individuals and companies alike are eager to gain CAD proficiency though they have only a sketchy idea of what it can do and what its repercussions will be.

Once this sizeable investment of time, effort, and money has been made, they soon become aware that things are not as they thought they would be: expectations are not being realized, well-established procedures are no longer working, talented staff are being wasted, initial enthusiasm has disappeared, costs are high, and benefits are hard to find.

These and many more problems arise when the CAD system is regarded as just another new piece of office technology, like a photocopier, requiring little more than a technical manual. The fact is, CAD does not just add something to a business but radically changes the way it works. The repercussions will permeate through to all areas of an organization effecting individual job demarcations and departmental interaction.

An awareness of this iconoclasm in the design office and an ability to deal successfully with it will enhance working procedures dramatically. Ignorance, on the other hand, will lead to disruptive and damaging consequences.

Who Should Read This Book

Anyone wishing to exploit CAD techniques as a means to an end rather than an end in itself will find this book of value, whether they are a Company Director considering investing in it or a designer designing with it.

It is written for people involved in design who are not interested in technology per se but rather in how technology can be used to help them. Its message is applicable in all the fields of work where CAD is found—architecture, civil engineering, manufacturing, graphics, engineering, product design, and so on. It is also of great use to those taking a more specialist interest in CAD and, to a lesser extent, those involved in the more general field of information technology management.

Whatever the area of discussion, I do not write as if for a specialist in any field (that is, a CAD specialist or a specialist in the topic being discussed at the time). For instance, you do not need to be an accountant to perceive what is written in the Financial Management part of the book.

Neither is it necessary for the reader to be familiar with a particular version or release of software; it will remain relevant and valuable as new software appears on the market. In fact, it is not even tied to CAD. Similar problems and opportunities face companies using many forms of IT and business software. This book is certainly useful to these people, though it is written primarily with the design business in mind.

I do not cover purchasing and installing computer systems. Nor do I discuss CAD operating techniques. Occasionally, when it is appropriate to refer to these matters, the technical terms and CAD commands that are used are generic. Any discussion on software and hardware concentrates on the reasoning behind it rather than simply reviewing equipment. That sort of information is available from many sources.

The chief members in the group of readers for whom this book is written are as follows.

The Company Director

Senior management and company directors wishing to gain an understanding of CAD will not be satisfied by an eye-catching display of computer-generated images at an exhibition or demonstration—no matter how impressive it may seem. Nor can the limited viewpoint of the CAD operator and the technical salesperson offer the necessary insight. Their prime concern is meeting business objectives.

This book provides an independent and broad view of the role design technology can play in doing just that. For example, it explains the ways in which CAD can be exploited, the financial justification, and the potential pitfalls.

The CAD Manager

Somewhere in the middle of the company hierarchy is the person charged with the task of managing the CAD facility. Soon after beginning their duties they discover that it is not like being responsible for any other company department. It involves taking new approaches to many of the ingrained office practices that will make many others in the company feel uneasy.

The pages of this book will prepare, guide, and inspire anyone with this responsibility by helping them (for example) implement a coherent CAD policy, overcome uncooperative attitudes toward CAD, and find, keep, and motivate the best CAD staff.

The CAD user

The scope of the specialist CAD operator is too often rather limited. Their chief interest is with the constantly evolving capabilities of the CAD system. This is quite understandable, and more than sufficient for most people to want to bother themselves about.

The designers using CAD can also find themselves limited in their vision. CAD is a complete design solution and should not be used simply as an electronic drawing board as is often the case.

I will discuss topics that reach out beyond the user and computer to more general concerns, that is, the sort of concerns that will appeal to anyone who is remotely interested in the broader perspective. In fact, this book can offer the CAD user career as well as mind enhancement. For example, I address such matters as the qualities that constitute the ideal CAD user, effective training to improve skills, and the extent of CAD's full design potential.

The Technical Consultant

Commonly, the same companies that supply CAD products also offer additional services to their clients such as technical support contracts and specialist advice. In addition, full-time consultants exist who earn their living by helping others to utilize their CAD investment. All of these people, whatever their field of specialty, will benefit by studying this book and keeping it by their side. It will allow them to offer expertise that encompasses not just the software and hardware but broader issues such as workload management, finance, and training.

Students

There are various educational courses where one will encounter CAD and its practical application. Many relevant degree courses exist, such as "Design and Technology." In fact, students studying many subjects whose title includes any of the following words are likely to be able to benefit from this book at some stage: Design, CAD, Engineering, Technology, Business, Management.

The business of training seminars is a competitive one in the field of CAD. This includes one-to-one tuition and large classes held at educational establishments. Both those preparing the course material and students attending the course could use this book to give themselves an edge over the competition. Nowadays it is not sufficient to simply know how to use CAD; one must know how to apply it. Similarly, those not attending courses but still wishing to learn could benefit greatly from this book. For example, a designer reared on the drawing board may be put off CAD by the seemingly prerequisite computer knowledge. This person will find the chapters that follow an informative guide to modern design techniques, not computing, with technical references kept to a minimum.

How to Use This Book

The chapters of the book are divided into nine distinct parts. Each part is sufficiently isolated from the others to allow them to be read independently and in any order.

At the end of each chapter there is a "what to do" list. The intention of these lists is to provide pointers to the key elements of each chapter and not a detailed, comprehensive agenda.

In many cases, these lists appear to be written for one specific group of readers; however, they should be interpreted for all. For example, a point on a "what to do" list may seem as if it is only relevant to the CAD Manager when it says

- Implement a staff-training program

but it should be interpreted by a CAD User as

- Get on-staff-training program

and by a Company Director as

- Authorize a staff-training program.

Throughout this book, the following expressions are used as an abbreviation for a wider interpretation:

CAD Manager: The person in a company who champions the cause of CAD and is responsible for its application.

Designers: Those using CAD or manual drawing methods in their work. This would refer to designers, architects, engineers, draftspeople, for example.

Designs: All output from the CAD Department, Drawing Office, Design Studio, and such.

Summary of Contents

Here is a brief summary of the issues tackled in each part of the book and the contents of each chapter:

Part 1: Management Effective CAD management and how it brings about the successful utilization and integration of the technology.

Chapter 1: Management and Technology The power and influence of the "Hybrid" manager — a person combining both technological understanding and business acumen.

Chapter 2: Job Specifications of the CAD Manager A description of the numerous managerial, technical, and clerical tasks involved in effective CAD management. By taking on these duties, the CAD Manager frees designers to concentrate on designing, optimize CAD effectiveness, and allow potential opportunities to be exploited.

Part 2: Fundamentals The varied and numerous opportunities of CAD and the obstacles that must be overcome for its potential to be realized.

Chapter 3: What's So Good about CAD? A clear and concise examination of the CAD advantage. Most people are aware only of a fraction of the potential opportunity that CAD presents; this chapter covers 30 chief benefits.

Chapter 4: Building on Initial Enthusiasm How to maintain the momentum of interest and enthusiasm that was present when CAD first entered the office.

Chapter 5: Overcoming Negative Attitudes Specific reasons for disgruntlement among the workforce and appropriate solutions. People, as a rule, do not welcome modern technology encroaching on working methods that have served satisfactorily for many years. As this is precisely what occurs when CAD technology is introduced into the workplace it is not surprising that certain negative feelings arise.

Part 3: Implementation CAD's role, range, and reach throughout the company.

Chapter 6: The Role of the CAD Department The way that CAD is put into practice. The approach taken should be clearly defined and understood by everyone. There are two routes to follow: (a) a CAD bureau within the company, with dedicated computer terminals operated by CAD specialists, providing a service to the designers, and (b) a fully integrated policy where the CAD facility is a tool used by designers as an integral part of their day-to-day activity.

Chapter 7: The Working Environment The siting of the CAD facility in the office and the users' working conditions. Both have a dramatic effect on job satisfaction and productivity.

Chapter 8: Broadening CAD's Range How the generation of CAD data can extend beyond the core system. This development can follow many routes, the three primary ones being Networks, Modems, and Data Transfer.

Chapter 9: Exploiting CAD Throughout the Business Successful data management that allows every area of activity to benefit from the CAD data. The companywide repercussions of the CAD system must not be restricted by viewing it in isolation.

Part 4: Staff What makes an ideal CAD user? How do you recruit them? What motivates them?

Chapter 10: The Ideal CAD User The qualities that define a successful computer-aided designer. They will in turn allow the CAD department, and then the whole company, to develop and prosper.

Chapter 11: Recruitment and Assessment The application forms, interviews, and hands-on sessions that are used to recruit and assess CAD staff.

Chapter 12: Staff Motivation What CAD users want from their job and the all-around benefits that will result when they get it.

Part 5: Training How staff can improve their skills and how managers can make the most of their staff.

Chapter 13: The Case for Training How training that is justified like any other investment not only improves workforce skills, but also accomplishes business objectives.

Chapter 14: Prerequisites for Effective Training How not to waste a training opportunity. To ensure its effectiveness there are preliminary requirements to consider.

Chapter 15: Training Programs The numerous ways to receive training; videotapes, software, books, manuals, distance learning, seminars, in-house courses, and training establishments offering a varied range of structured courses.

Part 6: The Workload The procedures and practices, such as data archiving and drawing standards, that any successful CAD practice must adhere to.

Chapter 16: Input The assessment of input data prior to use. CAD allows information from a variety of sources to be incorporated into the design work. To avoid a lack of conformity there are a number of assessment procedures to be followed.

Chapter 17: Resources Evaluation of resources, whether hardware, software, or the people using it. This will indicate any deficiency that may hinder the successful completion of a project.

Chapter 18: Data The working methods that must be known and formalized to ensure data integrity, that is, that the CAD-related data remains reliable and secure.

Chapter 19: Scheduling The planning that must take place to avoid arguments over who does what and when on the CAD system. Elements of the project that are most suited to CAD techniques can be identified and neatly slotted into a work schedule.

Chapter 20: Drawing The style and standards of the drawing. This is essential to create clarity and coherence between individual designers throughout a project. To a large extent, style and standards can be preset in prototype drawings.

Chapter 21: Output The verification of the final output from the CAD system, either in paper or electronic form. This may be carried out independently by simply looking over the drawing or by performing a set of test calculations.

Part 7: Project Planning The sort of planning that has evolved over many years and is just as necessary today to avoid wasted time, effort, and resources.

Chapter 22: A Route Plan for CAD Projects A preset "route" for a project to follow. From input of data to output of finished product project planning is essential for error-ridden work to be avoided.

Chapter 23: Project Management Software Software-based facilities that can assist the planning of a project.

Part 8. Quality Assurance (QA) QA procedures that make sense whether a company intends to be officially accredited with a QA standard or not.

Chapter 24: QA and CAD The stages involved in implementing a QA policy that will result in a working practice free of the self-induced crises that plague many design offices. This is applicable whether or not you are, or wish to be, officially accredited for QA.

Chapter 25: Preparing CAD QA Policy How a list of documents can be drawn up to comprise a QA policy for the CAD installation.

Chapter 26: The Operating Procedures Documents Examples of and comments on actual CAD QA documents. They describe what is done, when, and by whom as well as how it is checked, accepted, and recorded.

Chapter 27: The Drawing Procedures Manual The QA drawing standards for CAD that define an acceptable "template" to which all designers in a company will work.

Part 9: Financial Management Identifying and accounting for the costs and returns of CAD.

Chapter 28: Investment and Returns The financial justification of the CAD investment.

Chapter 29: Cost Management Monitoring costs and setting charges. Incorporating a charge to a client for the CAD facility requires the identification of actual costs and the time over which those costs are to be recovered. Strict cost management can lead to the development of a CAD "Cost Center"— a financially independent business within a business.

CAD at Work

Management

Too often a computer-aided design system is purchased in the mistaken belief that it is some kind of magic drawing board that just needs to be plugged in and left alone to work its miracles.

This belief is soon shattered when people realize that a CAD system is nothing more than a box of electronic components and needs human intervention to bring it to life. The skills of the CAD operator allow the facility to be utilized, but it is management that allows it to be applied effectively.

Effective management of the CAD facility involves a combination of technological understanding and managerial know-how. When these qualities are embodied in a single person, they are known as a "Hybrid" Manager.

The Hybrid Manager as CAD Manager holds an influential position within the company with numerous managerial, technical, and clerical tasks that are unique to the role.

Taking on these responsibilities will allow the CAD system to dramatically enhance the business of design, not by magic but by management.

1

Management and Technology

Technology presents an enormous opportunity, though actually exploiting this potential by putting technological advances into the work environment often proves to be troublesome. This is particularly noticeable in the design industry, where the technological revolution is changing established working practices so completely that many companies are having great difficulty coming to terms with it.

So what should be done? There are three possible courses of action:

- Ignore the technology.

- Bring in the technology and see what happens.

- Bring in the technology and manage it appropriately.

This chapter covers the last alternative.

A Revolution in the Workplace

In recent years we have witnessed the phenomenal rise of computer technology, as it has progressed from bulky and unwieldy equipment, rarely found outside the scientific research laboratories, to handy and adaptable personalized tools. Computers are no longer the mind-boggling, futuristic wonders they once were; now they are as commonplace and as indispensable as pen and paper.

Everyone is touched by computer technology to some degree. We are all quite happy with the computerized data processing that takes place in daily life (such as depositing and withdrawing money from a bank). As computers become accepted in just about every known field of business, the proportion of the workforce that is computer-literate is increasing. In the workplace, the spread of computer technology from straightforward number crunching into other areas has provided new possibilities for all.

The move from the specialist to the everyday worker has placed an enormous amount of power in the hands of individuals within a company. For instance, publishing—from conception to production—would once have taken many people much time using a great deal of equipment. The whole process can now be accomplished quickly by one person with a computer. In other words, the computer presents the opportunity to place the means of production and distribution at the fingertips of an independent worker, just as Karl Marx had hoped for. However, it has come about by a technological revolution geared toward satisfying the needs of the individual rather than by the route he envisaged.

The force with which this revolution has swept through the design world has proved to be iconoclastic. It is not just a matter of computers replacing drawing boards; the whole design process must change.

The spectrum of computer-aided design applications is a very broad one. Consider such diverse areas as the layout of microchip circuits, seating plans for multistory office blocks, supertanker construction, and textile design. In all these areas, computer-aided design has become the norm. In this wide-ranging business, as elsewhere, people are attempting to come to terms with the technological opportunity. Unfortunately, for many companies, it is more of a technological nightmare.

Why is it that, while some organizations utilize and integrate technology to enhance their working practice, others struggle on, unsure of what they are doing and why they are doing it?

The answer lies with management.

The Most Effective Type of Manager

Salespersons are too fond of emphasizing the user-friendliness of computer technology while playing down the need for any ongoing intervention. This leads to the implementation of CAD systems without any provision being made for management. User-friendly does not mean magic. If the enormous potential is to be exploited, it can only come about by effective management.

So what sort of person is capable of creating and seeing through a winning CAD policy? There are three types of manager to choose from: the Computer Whiz Kid, the Departmental Manager, and the Hybrid Manager. The first two are the most common choices, as they are both solutions that present themselves with minimal effort. However, it is the third type of manager that will provide the most effective results.

The Computer Whiz Kid

There is usually one person in an organization responsible for getting the technological ball rolling. Within the confines of the office, this person may be regarded as an expert. Considering the level of technological ignorance among those who hold the purse strings, it isn't surprising that this person's opinion carries a lot of weight. Consequently, once the CAD system is implemented, it's an obvious next step to place the Computer Whiz Kid in charge of it.

Whiz Kids can follow the manuals, get the system up and running, and be able to talk to the supplier using the appropriate jargon. They might even be able to use the equipment, in a superficial sort of way. Once the Whiz has created a few squiggles, squares, and circles on the screen and sent them to the plotter where they manifest on paper, everyone will be suitably impressed and think that they have cracked the puzzle.

Then reality hits. Problems, disruption, confusion, missed deadlines — panic!

Investing in a CAD system is not like buying a new lamp for the office where all one needs to know is how to switch it on and change a burnt-out bulb. As mentioned already, the whole design process must change. There is little possibility of accomplishing this if the person directing the proceedings is someone without any companywide business acumen. A more suitable role for this type of person would be Systems Manager, possibly working beneath the CAD Manager.

The Departmental Manager

Another course of action takes place when senior management is aware of the need for effective CAD management and decides to treat it like any other department and appoint a Departmental Manager.

This person, with proven managerial skills, selected by the board, will view the CAD investment with a more businesslike eye than the previous candidate. She will organize staff and allocate workloads, monitor budgets, and report to the board.

Soon, however, the board will realize that CAD is not just an electronic drawing board. It presents new opportunities and new problems and specialist skills are needed to deal with them. A Departmental Manager will lack knowledge of CAD techniques and consequently be unable to ensure the effective application of the new technology.

The Hybrid Manager

This expression was brought to public attention initially by Peter Keen and then defined further in 1989 by Professor Michael Earl and Dr.

Figure 1-1. The "Hybrid" Manager.

David Skyrme, who used it to describe people with strong technical skills and adequate business knowledge, or vice versa (see Fig. 1-1).

These characters are evolving and appearing in more and more companies. They are technologically experienced, while possessing business and managerial know-how. They are thoroughly versed in the companywide repercussions of CAD technology and at ease among the senior management echelons.

CAD Management must never be treated as a purely technical role or limited to basic departmental organization. The Hybrid Manager combines both technical and management skills, providing a potent cocktail whose influence will strengthen as time passes. This is the most valuable blend of skills today's manager can possess. If a "hybrid" is given the job of CAD Manager, he has it in his power to lead the whole company forward.

His ability to generate and communicate ideas, his general management experience and understanding of the design process, as well as an understanding of Computer-Aided Design, makes the Hybrid Manager a valuable commodity in the company.

Hybrid Managers are evolving naturally to suit the modern working environment. When they cannot be found, they can be created. Many large companies have management training courses specifically to turn Computer Whiz Kids and Departmental Managers into Hybrid Managers.

The CAD Manager needs to be strong and forthright to maintain their position in the company, often when others feel their toes being tread upon. For instance, it is not uncommon for conflict to occur between the existing Drawing Office Manager and the new CAD Manager. To fulfill his unique role, a CAD Manager needs to be a Hybrid Manager.

In the not-too-distant future, as this managerial evolution has progressed further, terms such as CAD Manager will have disappeared to be replaced by just "Manager," possibly prefixed with "Design." That is, all managers will be (to some extent) Hybrid Managers.

Power and Influence of the Hybrid/CAD Manager

Sooner or later (usually sooner) a design company that attempts to exist as a traditional island in a technological ocean will have to face up to the world as it really is. Nowadays, technology is an inextricable part of the design process and its influence permeates throughout the whole company and beyond. The range and the reach of the potential benefits of design technology are enormous, as we shall see later in this book.

The emergence of Hybrid Managers in the design business has particular importance, as they possess knowledge and control of this vital technology. This places them in a very powerful position, as control of technology is a significant proportion of control of the company.

When technological responsibilities are delegated, power and influence are passed down the line. If senior management abdicates responsibility completely for technology, it will be unable to lead its company through today's business environment. This is why the CAD Manager's role is so vital and the concerns of this book so pertinent to a design company's success or failure.

What to Do

- Implement a CAD strategy that is management-led, from the top of the company.
- Make CAD, and the strategy, a companywide issue.
- Allow CAD to change the culture of the company.
- Utilize Hybrid Managers — if necessary, create them through specialized training courses.

2

Job Specifications
of the CAD Manager

In Chapter 1, we saw the importance of identifying the right type of manager for the CAD investment. In this chapter, we'll take a look at the CAD Manager's tasks and responsibilities.

We'll examine a point-by-point checklist of activities that comprise the job specifications — 34 points in all. If the role is not identified and suitably filled, many of these activities will not even be recognized — never mind carried out. Yet, after reading this chapter, you'll be hard-pressed to imagine how a company could ever function without this character.

By taking on these tasks and responsibilities, the CAD Manager frees designers from the frustrating and time-consuming chores that often hinder their work. The CAD process will be optimized to maximize effectiveness, and designers will be able to focus their efforts on what they do best — designing.

The tasks and responsibilities are grouped according to three distinct areas of activity: managerial, technical, and clerical.

Managerial

The CAD Manager does not fit into the old design company structure and can easily become detached, without the authority to make things happen. The CAD Manager must have sufficient authority to initiate and implement policy rather than merely suggest it to others. Pioneering new working practices is only possible when possessing the seniority to direct events.

If the CAD Manager's role is not granted such a high standing, then the authority must be achieved by association — by forming a partnership with someone at a senior level as demonstrated in Fig. 2-1. There

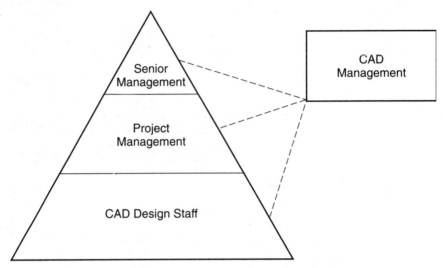

Figure 2-1. The position of CAD management in the company structure.

is usually one Director that championed the cause of design technology at board level sufficiently for it to be introduced in the first place (ideally, the Managing Director). Forming a partnership with this person would mean directives issued by the CAD Manager would bear the authority of the Managing Director.

Inform directors about CAD capabilities

Senior management must be familiar with what is happening at the CAD "workface." This may be accomplished by a combination of methods such as formalized management awareness training sessions, casual demonstrations of applications and working practices, and official reports prepared by the CAD Manager on potential developments.

Initiate CAD policy to fulfill company needs

An awareness and understanding of the company's business objectives requires liaison at senior level. A fully utilized and strategically applied CAD department can make a substantial contribution to the achievement of these objectives.

Apply specialist knowledge to budgeting

It is easy to be drawn into the purchase of white elephants by impressive but superficial demonstrations and salespeople that are only interested in fulfilling their quotas. CAD equipment is generally expensive, so it is absolutely essential that all investments and costs are managed with professional insight.

Communicate with divisional managers

Any reluctance by Project Managers toward fully committing their work to CAD must be overcome. To achieve this, they must be continually informed and educated on the benefits that CAD can bring to their own projects.

Be involved at a project's inception

In the initial stages of a project, it is vital that there is someone there to champion the cause of the CAD facility. Underrepresentation will be detrimental to the project and could harm future prospects.

Schedule the workload

An organized approach to CAD usage is preferable to the anarchic alternative. A planned schedule that clarifies who works on what machine, and when and on what job, must be devised and constantly maintained by the CAD Manager in conjunction with Project Managers.

Implement quality procedures

Computers inevitably enforce an element of standardization and regimentation. This must be developed and formalized, and, if one exists, incorporated into the company's Quality Assurance policy.

Stimulate motivation, innovation, and enthusiasm

The introduction of CAD into the workplace adds a new element to the workforce—CAD Users. The CAD Manager needs to induce a positive ethos into the users that will encourage the full exploitation of the investment.

Bring about and measure effectiveness

As for any costly investment, it is an essential ongoing task to monitor the efficiency of the CAD system and to analyze its repercussions throughout the organization.

Create a CAD environment

To plan appropriate working conditions requires an awareness of the unique nature of CAD. Computers cannot simply be sited as if they were drawing boards. Also, location has a significant influence on the role CAD plays in a company.

Manage the system's installation and growth

A planned and orderly approach must be taken to the development and subsequent handling of the CAD system. A coherent strategy is much more effective than a "here and now" approach that stores up trouble for the future.

Be the sole contact for referrals

It is essential that anyone inside or outside the company with a CAD query or comment knows precisely who to speak to and where to find them, rather than having to deal with whomever happens to be sitting near the telephone when it rings.

Technical

In an earlier life, the CAD Manager was frequently a CAD Whiz Kid. This technological background is valuable for many aspects of the job, when analyzing a project's suitability for CAD allocation, for example, as well as for the more obvious technical matters. It may be possible to delegate some of these tasks to the current Whiz Kid, or, as in some larger organizations, to a Systems Manager, thus freeing the CAD Manager to concentrate solely on the managerial responsibilities.

Explain what the technology can and cannot do

It is a bizarrely common misapprehension that a computer will perform any task that a computer has ever been seen to do—at the mere push of a button! Clarification of how the CAD system can best be utilized is needed to combat such ignorance and to ensure that its true benefits are exploited.

Identify all applications for the CAD system

The possibilities that lie beyond the "electronic drawing board" view of CAD must be seized. It can be surprisingly difficult to come to terms with and exploit the enormous potential opportunity that CAD puts in the hands of the individual designer.

Integrate CAD companywide

It is important that every department benefits from the store of information held in the CAD database. This task is made easier as computerization spreads throughout the whole company structure.

Facilitate access for less-skilled users

System customization and the use of add-on packages can open up the system to a broader audience. For example, simplifying partial access for non-CAD staff would allow Project Managers to view progress of their project on-screen.

Establish work procedures

Passwords, filenaming standards, backing up, and so on provide a reliable framework of procedures within which work can progress without setbacks. These procedures may be documented and, in some cases, incorporated into the system so that they take place automatically.

Standardize settings

A standardized approach to drawing entities, text, and dimension styles (for instance) provides a unified approach that allows many designers working on large and long-lasting projects to operate in a coherent and harmonious way. Again, these standards can often be incorporated into the CAD system permanently.

Solve operational problems

CAD expertise, general system knowledge, and familiarity with working practices are valuable skills that enable the CAD Manager to act as the first stop for any operational queries.

Organize training and monitor progress

Training is essential in any dynamic business. To provide permanent worthwhile benefits, it must be ongoing, targeted, and effective.

Utilize time prior to a project

There are many things that can be done to enhance the CAD design process before it gets underway. A solid foundation can be prepared (for example) by creating standard symbols and repeated drawing elements, and setting standard text styles, hatch patterns, and layers.

Apply customization techniques

The CAD system should be tailored to the needs of individual users and projects. The reward for such forward thinking is a significant increase in the speed and profitability of CAD.

Rectify unfulfilled potential within the system

Weakness of the CAD set-up and wasted opportunities must be identified and rectified. These can result from a number of sources. They cause frustration among users and dissatisfaction among senior management.

Keep abreast of what's on the market

Design technology is an industry developing at a phenomenal rate. To keep up-to-date, it is worthwhile going to exhibitions, seminars, and user groups, reading magazines, and researching new software.

Implement computer "housekeeping"

Regular "memory management" and "debugging" of the memory banks is a classic example of prevention being the best form of cure. When a glitch does occur it is often too late to do anything about it.

Clerical

There will inevitably be an amount of administration to contend with. This increases dramatically when the role encompasses elements of companywide organizational schemes such as Quality Assurance and financial management. Both of these topics are discussed in later chapters of the book.

Report on CAD activity

Keeping the board informed of current and proposed developments allows CAD to be involved in company strategy discussions. Preparing progress reports also serves to inform the rest of the workforce about something they may well be both ignorant and wary of.

Canvass opinion from all sectors of the workforce

It is important to keep in touch with individual and departmental requirements by means of questionnaires, newsletters, discussion groups, and so on. This will benefit all concerned.

Publish workload information

As well as clarifying and spreading awareness of the workload schedule, this is useful propaganda for keeping the whole company aware of activity in the CAD department.

Document all standards and procedures

Introducing CAD into the workplace alters the way a company works. This incurs new procedures that must be identified and made known to all those concerned.

Provide guidance notes where needed

Issuing workable guidelines and instructions to every user, or placing them by every machine, will prevent many avoidable mishaps. These notes should be considered as a backup rather than the primary source of information.

Oversee support and maintenance

A water-tight contract must guarantee breakdown recovery and support at times of need. The CAD Manager must be the sole contact, from initial negotiation throughout the life of the contract.

Centralize all CAD literature

Access to a well-managed collection of manuals and drawing libraries is a necessary requirement for the designer's work.

Organize the provision of all materials

Adequate and reliable supplies of a suitable quality and price are essential prerequisites for the CAD design process. This would include floppy disks, plotting media, screen cleaner, and so on.

Act as a focal point among CAD users

By facilitating the development and exchange of ideas and information between individual designers, the CAD Manager acts as a catalyst for the enhancement of the working process.

What to Do

- Inform directors on the capabilities of CAD.
- Initiate CAD policy to fulfill company needs.
- Apply a specialist knowledge to budgeting.
- Communicate with divisional managers.
- Be involved at a project's inception.
- Schedule the workload.

- Implement quality procedures.
- Stimulate motivation, innovation, and enthusiasm.
- Bring about and measure effectiveness.
- Create a CAD environment.
- Manage the system's installation and growth.
- Be the sole contact for any CAD-related referrals.
- Explain what the technology can/cannot do.
- Identify all applications for the CAD system.
- Integrate CAD companywide.
- Facilitate access for less skilled users.
- Establish work procedures.
- Standardize settings.
- Solve operational problems.
- Organize training and monitor progress.
- Utilize time prior to a project.
- Apply customization techniques.
- Rectify unfulfilled potential within the system.
- Keep abreast of what's on the market.
- Implement computer "housekeeping."
- Report on CAD activity.
- Canvass opinion from all sectors of the workforce.
- Publish workload information.
- Document all standards and procedures.
- Provide guidance notes where needed.
- Oversee support and maintenance.
- Centralize all CAD literature.
- Organize the provision of all materials.
- Act as the focal point among CAD users.

2

Fundamentals

It is easy to be fooled into believing that technological progress is straightforward and painless. However, as you blindly speed down the futuristic highway, it is surprising how soon you can find yourself heading along the wrong road. After a while you begin to think, "This isn't how it was meant to be!"

There are three fundamental prerequisites for the successful application of design technology. Staying with the motoring analogy, we cannot hope to arrive at our destination unless:

- *We know where we are going before we set off.*
- *We know how to get there.*
- *We want to get there.*

CAD offers a tremendous opportunity. This part of the book explains the varied and numerous possibilities design technology presents, how they can be achieved, and how the practical and psychological obstacles that will be encountered on the way can be overcome.

3

What's So Good About CAD?

Before a company can fully exploit its CAD investment, it must be aware of all the possible opportunities it presents. This chapter covers numerous and varied capabilities of CAD that benefit both the design and management sides of a business.

Each capability mentioned has repercussions throughout the company. For instance, "data extraction" is demonstrated when (for example) a designer working on a department store project wants to ascertain the area covered by carpet. What was once an inaccurate or lengthy exercise can be accomplished almost instantaneously using CAD techniques, automatically extricating the required information from the CAD drawing. The same provision of design data can be used by management for budgeting and client liaison. Clearly, this CAD capability enhances the business as a whole and not just one particular part of it.

Each company has its own particular circumstances and corresponding uses for CAD. It is, therefore, impossible to list every specific advantage CAD brings to all businesses. The points raised in this chapter should be considered the core capabilities that can be built upon according to individual and company needs.

The contents of this chapter also constitute the reason we choose to use CAD over alternative methods of working. And, as we will see in Chapter 4, it provides propaganda ammunition with which to justify CAD to others so that they may also appreciate its usefulness. So, when anyone asks, "What's so good about CAD?", this is what you can tell them.

Speed

This is the advantage that most readily springs to mind. Even those poor souls that still think of CAD as an electronic drawing board can comprehend this one. Unfortunately, this is in fact not always true, as a basic two-dimensional CAD drawing is often no quicker (and sometimes slower) than the manual alternative. This fact can lead to an instant rejection of CAD by a disappointed Project Manager.

The true benefit of speed is noticeable when the initial drawing is adapted, modified, or used in some way. For example, it may be too small, so it can be scaled up in an instant; it may need repositioning, so it can be moved and rotated until satisfactory; it may then need to be repeated thirty times, equally spaced, along an 176.37 degree arc and superimposed on a drawing done fifteen months ago, so it can be "polar arrayed," then "inserted" into the old drawing, and—Presto!—it's done.

Experimenting with variations of the original is far faster with CAD than by hand. For instance, the designer can quickly see how an alteration to a building's floor plan will affect the electrical layout and modify it accordingly, or perhaps notice the extent to which the capacity of a petrol tanker can be increased without modifying the livery design.

A vast array of editing commands are available to modify existing CAD work. However, the nearest thing a manual designer has to an editing tool is the eraser, which simply and untidily returns him back to a blank sheet.

In any project, initial drawings evolve through a series of revisions, culminating in the satisfactory end result. The time taken to alter a drawing each time a revision is made accounts for a large proportion of the total time spent on the project. CAD reduces this time dramatically, thus reducing costs and time delays. Major revisions that would otherwise mean virtually starting from scratch on a new piece of paper can be made "on the fly" with minimal disturbance.

The benefit of speed does not necessarily mean that less time is spent drawing. Frequently it means that the same amount of time is spent, but more is achieved. In other words, time is spent on important aspects of a project, such as scrutiny, analysis, and exploring ideas.

A common question is, "If CAD is so essential, how did the designers of the past get by without it?" The simple response is that the likes of Brunel and Wren would have had to rely on swarms of assistants. Every aspect of the design would be subject to scrutinization by technicians, mathematicians, and experts from many fields. The time involved in pursuing a single idea would have been phenomenal. Compare this to CAD, which allows the designer to investigate numerous concepts in an afternoon.

Neatness

The use of CAD undoubtedly enhances the general presentation of a drawing.

Who can forget the bad old days of smudged pencil lines, fingerprints, pencils disappearing down compass holes, creased drawings, sneezing over the drawing, and so on?

No such problems exist with CAD, although it is true that good design work is often let down by an inadequate plotter. Even so, this drawback is easily overcome, unlike the others that are part and parcel of the manual design process.

As well as the drawing, nongraphic elements must be considered, such as text and dimensioning. CAD makes it possible to take a constant and coherent approach that just would not be possible manually. Although some designers may take great pride in their hand lettering, there is no place for self-indulgence in business. CAD is neater, and that is what is important.

Drawing presentation is something covered in more detail in Chapter 20.

Accuracy

CAD is 100% accurate. This, compared to the error-prone manual approach, is a fundamental dissimilarity between the two design methods. A manual designer draws something on paper, then writes in the "real size" dimension. A CAD designer, however, works in the "real size" (scale 1:1), and the dimension he enters will genuinely be that of what has been drawn. That is, rightly or wrongly, the drawing is accurate, whereas the manual designer will have the right dimension no matter how inaccurate his drawing!

The margin of error is greater with the manual approach because of the reason just given and also because pencils and rulers can never be used with guaranteed precision. For example, imagine two designers creating the same 1:100 scale site plan, one with CAD and the other with pencil and paper. It has been decided to erect columns in a ten-meter-square grid pattern throughout the plan. One of the columns encroaches by 10mm on space allocated for a doorway, thus preventing the door from opening fully. CAD is 100% accurate and so this designer spots the problem easily. The manual designer, however, is simply unable to draw to that degree of accuracy. A 10mm discrepancy corresponds to 0.1mm on the drawing, far smaller than the degree of error inherent in that drawing method. Even if both designers suspect a problem, it is only the CAD designer that can accurately verify and analyze the situation and modify the design accordingly.

Even when using aids, such as a grid, to position a line on a drawing, the accuracy of the CAD system surpasses that of a hand-drawn grid by a long way. True, it might still be a grid, but it is a hand-drawn grid and a hand-drawn line. This is even more evident when drawing a line intended to be tangential to a curve. Relying on eyes and a steady hand will give a reasonable-looking tangent, but not the guaranteed accurate one that CAD can provide by "snapping" to the actual tangent point on the curve.

To conclude this point, CAD results in fewer errors and hence less rework. Consequently, time is not wasted on impractical drawings but rather spent constructively on drawings that can be developed without repeated problems presenting themselves at the manufacturing stage.

Layering

Most CAD systems have a way of splitting a drawing up into component layers of information that can be added or removed from the working drawing. The name given to this varies from system to system.

Similarly, elements of a manual drawing can be isolated from the rest of the image by adding or removing layers of acetates. Each sheet contains a different group of elements, the whole drawing being displayed when all sheets are in place.

Compared to acetates, CAD provides a greatly more flexible tool with a host of controls over each layer. This in demonstrated in Fig. 3-1 where a drawing created with AutoCAD AEC Release 5 software has its layers manipulated during a CAD session.

There are numerous ways in which this facility can assist the designer. For instance, design alternatives can be layered, then viewed as part of the overall drawing, to investigate their suitability. Rejected options can still remain, but on "invisible" layers made visible again, should they be wanted in the future.

As well as enhancing the design process, layering saves time and effort. For example, when the basic structure of a building has been drawn, it is not necessary to repeat it any more in the project. The same image can provide the background layer for the electrical details, the circulation diagram, the flooring plan, and so on—each held on their own layers but merged with the main structural layer when required.

Viewpoints

It is a simple and almost instantaneous procedure to create what would be seen of a CAD drawing from any one of an infinite number of viewpoints.

This capability is another fundamental difference between manual and CAD design techniques. With manual techniques, what you draw

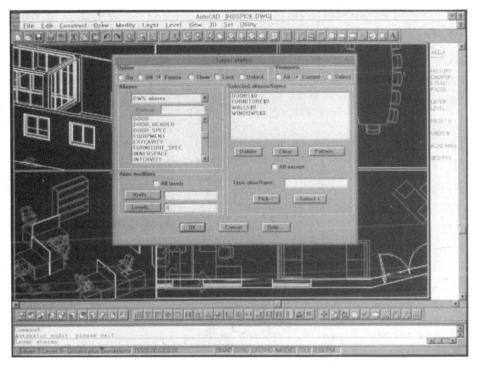

Figure 3-1. Using layers in a CAD drawing. *(Autodesk Ltd.)*

is what you get—as simple as that. If you want a particular view, you need to draw it. With CAD, however, what you draw is just the starting point. Once the initial image has been created, the designer can choose "how" to look at it.

For instance, a straightforward plan can also be viewed in axonometric form, with controllable perspective, without any additional drawing work needing to be done. Or, small areas may be looked at in an enhanced view to show detailed work, all presented alongside one another—again with no additional drawing work.

The possibilities extend further when three-dimensional CAD images are involved. That is dealt with next.

Virtual Models

The benefits of a product model created in the workshop can often be provided more successfully by a three-dimensional CAD image.

Three-dimensional CAD work is more akin to model-making than drawing. CAD designers move around their creation, viewing and modifying as they go, yet the three-dimensional model does not actually exist: all that does exist is a computer database.

From a single 3-D "model," all elevations can be viewed, plus viewpoints from any point in 3-D space, internally and externally, with various degrees of perspective. The time-consuming (not to mention boring) manual task of mechanically constructing a perspective on the drawing board can now be forgotten.

During work on most projects, there will be a stage in the design process where it becomes necessary to actually build a full-size prototype to identify the practical problems of the design. CAD doesn't make this step unnecessary, but a CAD model on the computer can provide solutions to many of the queries that the full-size model is intended to answer, such as "If someone stood here, will they be able to see over there?" and "How far away can a person be and still see this sign?" These questions can be answered and the design modified accordingly in a procedure taking minutes, without the designer having to get out of his chair.

If we take this a step further, by quickly displaying an appropriate sequence of views, one after another, an animated effect can be created, providing a virtual walk through a building. This capability is valuable to the designer and the client and can be achieved without any additional drawing work and probably in less time than it would take a manual designer to render a single drawing.

Reduced External Involvement

Many of the tasks previously necessitating the services of additional staff, often from outside the company, can now be accomplished using CAD. Consequently, it is quite possible for a CAD designer to see a project through from beginning to end without the need to refer to specialist external services, such as visualizers.

Reducing this superfluous interference brings a coherence to the design process that can only enhance the work being done. Understanding of the project and the motivation in tackling it are maintained. More and more external involvement with a project inevitably means that understanding and motivation suffer as they are passed down the line, being diluted at every stage.

Symbol Libraries

Common components of a drawing can be compiled and accessed via a menu during a CAD session. This allows instant placement of the chosen element into the drawing, with the opportunity to align and resize if necessary.

Symbol libraries can be purchased or developed in-house. They can be created gradually over time or prior to a piece of work. Architectural symbols are commonly accessed using this technique, and elements relating to a project (such as a specific style of furniture) are often grouped into libraries.

For example, the AEC (Architectural, Engineering and Construction) package that accompanies AutoCAD provides a menu system offering easy access to a vast array of predrawn entities in two and three dimensions and symbols such as structural, sanitary, electrical, lighting, service, furniture, appliance, and site.

Symbol libraries, particularly those developed in-house, are a valuable commodity. They can be kept for future use, copied to subcontractors to maintain project standardization, or even sold to other companies working on similar projects.

Global Editing

CAD techniques allow certain modifications to be performed across a whole drawing in a single action. That is, CAD can work "globally," irrespective of how large the job. What this means in practice is that a designer can change the appearance or characteristics of a recurring element in a drawing in one quick move. This may be performed on a drawing, across a project, or even a whole lifetime of work.

For example, imagine if a symbol that had been used countless times throughout a large project was found to be confusingly similar to another and subsequently needed to be altered. Now imagine having to perform such an awesome task manually, erasing then redrawing the symbol in each occurrence. Such a task doesn't bear thinking about. Thanks to CAD, though, the appearance of the symbol can be "redefined" and each drawing updated automatically.

Preprogramming

It is possible to perform a number of tasks by simply initiating a programmed sequence of instructions. The program will then run, without anyone needing to be present.

For example, a number of commands could be batched together that will enter a drawing, zoom to its extents, plot it onto A4 paper, then save the drawing onto a floppy disk before repeating the procedure on the next drawing in the project. Or, as another example, an automated sequence may look at every drawing in the computer and alter the title box to show the company's new address.

Such examples rely on the accessibility of the CAD system to external programming. AutoCAD is excellent for this and provides the means to access any elements from the drawing database allowing it to be viewed, altered, or plotted out via programmed instructions.

Another application of programming is to customize the CAD system to suit the needs of the operator and the project. A simple example of this is a customized command menu that provides easy access to frequently used commands and functions to perform commonly requested procedures.

Intelligent Drawings

Thanks to a "brain" behind the drawing, complex calculations can be solved in an instant, and tasks that would once have been troublesome now become easy.

For example, if a peculiar shape in the flooring plans of a building needs to be covered with expensive tiles, the precise dimensions and areas must be known. CAD provides all the details of this shape—perimeter, area, center points, angles. If the surface area were found to be beyond that possible with the budget allocation, then adjustments can be made accordingly. This would be a very long-winded and tedious procedure using manual methods.

In addition to this data, created simultaneously with the drawing, further information can be implanted by the user. For instance, a simple rectangular representation of a desk drawn in an office layout plan can tell any number of things: size, type, supplier, cost, name of person sitting there, job title, extension number, and so on. This can all be tied to the desk "invisibly" until accessed—say, by clicking on the desk with the mouse.

Compare this "intelligence" to a "dumb" manual drawing.

Standardization

Some projects have components that are repeated throughout. For example, a multistory hotel might have everything from the electrical layout to the bath taps identical in every room.

CAD can guarantee that common components in a drawing will be exact replicas of each other.

Elements of a drawing can be represented by predrawn symbols that actually fit the dimensions of the thing they represent. There is no need to draw the same chair over and over again, or indicate its position with an inaccurate swirl of the pencil differing in size and shape each time one is drawn. With CAD realistic, standardized representations throughout a piece of work are possible.

Apart from benefiting the design process, this guarantee of standardization leads to lower manufacturing costs.

On large projects particularly, text styles, dimension styles, line weight, hatching, company logos, even note "bubbles," and so on, must be standardized. Manually this presents a major task—text inevitably varies in size and style from drafter to drafter. The situation is even worse when the project is spread over many months or years. CAD, on the other hand, remembers any standards and automatically implements them—even if it involved a new designer coming back to the project many years later. The "house style" will be evident by its unerring consistency, as it should be.

This has an added advantage too. Simplification by standardization often results in a reduction of the more mundane drawing work in a project. This subsequently raises enthusiasm among staff and encourages more creative work.

Organization

For some reason "designers" and "organization" are two words that don't go together. "Designers" and "chaos," on the other hand, do. However, that was when manual design methods were being used; now things are changing.

CAD working procedure inevitably incurs a degree of organization. All work must be named and stored in a designated place within the computer. Furthermore, aided by a little customization, organization within the drawing can be enforced so that even the most undisciplined member of the design team has to comply with certain drawing office rules.

This facility is particularly useful where many designers are involved in a project over long periods of time. Organizational procedures would normally be extremely difficult to maintain in this situation.

As a result of this enforced organization, and also to improve it, drawing file status, catalogs of projects, and so on can be printed for the benefit of both staff and management.

Quality Control

Quality Control (QC) describes the operation of satisfying the quality requirements of the final product. The order and regimentation that is involved in QC is inherent in CAD.

The inspection process, which is the essence of QC, is quicker because there are fewer errors with CAD. Inbuilt procedures that, for instance, automatically prompt the checker to "sign off" a drawing, mean that the process is a relatively smooth one that is easily incorporated into normal working practices.

Quality can be further controlled by other CAD features—for instance, filing, backing up, and archiving. These procedures provide a guarantee over the integrity of the CAD data. They are also particularly useful if there are disputes involving the work after completion.

Quality Assurance

Quality Assurance (QA) takes into account the overall planning and management of the business as well as the "product." Full commitment to the QA ideals can lead to official recognition with ISO 9000 or a similar recognized standard.

It is often the case that CAD leads the rest of the company along this path. In fact, for many companies, the predominant reason for choosing CAD in the first place is to improve the quality of their design process.

Common to all QA systems are feedback loops by which any shortcomings can be identified and rectified as soon as is possible. The capabilities of CAD dramatically reduce the time and effort involved in responding to the feedback.

CAD's relationship with QA is detailed in Part 8 of this book.

Data Extraction

CAD allows the designer access to more details of the design than would be possible with manual methods.

This is very useful when it comes to preparing documentation on a design—for, say, costing the design or specifying the number of bricks in a building. All of this design data can be extracted from a CAD drawing.

Most CAD systems are able to utilize the plentiful, relatively cheap, software packages that perform automatic documentation tasks quickly and easily. For example, a "Bill of Materials" program will examine at the drawing database, extricate relevant data on every element of the drawing, then translate and present it in a clear and readable form. Thus, the whole analysis and documentation task is performed quickly, easily, accurately, and automatically.

Incorporation of Others' CAD Data

Once you have a CAD system you can incorporate any work from somebody else's system into yours.

These days many clients have their own CAD system. So, as long as they give permission, this opens up a whole database of information, available by simply transferring it across onto your company's system. The CAD data can then be accessed and edited, plotted, or whatever you wish.

This is particularly useful at the outset of a project where it is helpful to incorporate initial "building blocks"—company logos or a building's existing architectural plan, for instance. This saves the time and effort that would otherwise be spent noncreatively simply by inputting the information before the design work can even begin.

Incorporation of Previous CAD Work

All previous CAD work is accessible and can be imported into current projects. Virtually all new design work utilizes knowledge and experience gained from past, similar projects. CAD allows this to be done with ease.

For example, if your company has a reputation as a designer of multistory carparks and is offering its services to a prospective client, you do not want to waste time repeating what was already done on previous projects. There will always be some common elements of the multistory carpark design process that can be transplanted directly from past work. There is no virtue in starting from scratch each time as if you were a novice.

The chores of preparing the basic structure, car flow diagrams, surface coverings, and so on can be avoided. The thought that went into the layout and positioning of specific items, such as a ticket machine, can be capitalized on now in the new project.

Similarly, this facility gives the designer the freedom to view, compare, and incorporate past workable solutions interactively while working on the current project.

Interpretation of Analysis Data

In the pre-CAD days of engineering, pages and pages of analysis results were collated on the product in question. These would then be handed to the drawing office for the laborious task of translating the piles of figures into drawings.

This is another example of how the designer was once inextricably linked to many tasks other than their specialty of creating drawings.

Now, thankfully, this data-handling process can be accomplished virtually automatically, allowing more constructive use of the designer's time.

Most modern methods of analysis use laser technology to create a long list of coordinates that only require a simple algorithm to translate into the language recognizable to a CAD system. In many fields, from geographical mapping to mass-produced industrial design, there are a range of facilities on the market that will analyze and present the required data in a CAD-friendly format.

Numerous Output Options

The final product of the CAD designer is best described as a computer database that can be output in a variety of ways. The word "drawing," when referring to CAD, does not do it justice. We usually think of a drawing as a flat image created by hand on a piece of paper and nothing more. This suitably sums up the output of the manual designer.

The most obvious way of outputting the CAD database is to plot the image onto paper. Here you can produce numerous identical copies, vary line color and thickness, plot at any scale, and so on. The choice of scale allows a design of, say, a chair to be printed out at full size to be used as a stencil by the manufacturer, at A4 to be faxed to the client, and a dozen times at A5 to be put in the designer's pocket to sketch on while in the pub at lunchtime.

Some of the other output options become apparent after a "transfer" of the CAD database has taken place. This is discussed under the next heading.

Transferable Data

CAD, as just mentioned, provides a database—not just a drawing. A drawing on a piece of paper is pretty well fixed, there is little more that can be done except copy the image onto other pieces of paper. A database, however, provides details of every element that constitutes the drawing.

There are plenty of possible uses for it, all involving some degree of data transference. For example, a plotter will translate all the vector information into the lines of a conventional-looking drawing. Alternatively, it could be incorporated into another database, from a CAD system either within or outside the company. This could involve transferring work to another graphics package for a specific treatment, or translating CAD images into a different format altogether.

The latter example may be useful when, after the design and drafting part of a project are over, the client requires that a manual be compiled. The presentation of this manual would best be handled by a dedicated desktop publishing package (DTP) rather than CAD. The database for each illustration can be transferred into the DTP machine so that images and text can be manipulated within the one software package.

Transferring CAD images onto 35mm film slides is particularly useful for presentations. Following on from that, animated CAD sequences can be transferred onto videotape to be viewed on a television.

CAD can be linked directly to manufacturing processes. For example, the same technology used in plotters is found in machines that will cut out the 2-D image that was created on the computer. Similar (but more costly) are their 3D equivalent.

The countless possibilities for converting database information into alternative forms cannot all be detailed here. Still, the number of applications is growing all the time and it is wise to regularly investigate developments in your particular field. Chances are that if you can think of an opportunity of utilizing your CAD database, it can be accomplished.

Data Storage and Retrieval

The ability to store work and retrieve it at a later date is a necessary part of responsible workload management. When CAD techniques are being used, the task is massively reduced as the equivalent of many A0 sheets of paper can be stored as data on a disk. This advantage becomes more apparent as projects grow.

Consider a project involving 200 drawings. There is no need for any of these to exist on paper. They can be stored on computer in a clear, organized structure.

There are clear benefits in the dramatic space savings of CAD data: easy access to old drawings, improved security, and so on. Throughout the project alternative versions can also be held should they be required at a later date. Work can be "backed up," giving a guarantee of security as well as peace of mind. The whole project can be put onto a tape or disks and stored offsite.

Simple programs can "compress" this data further allowing the whole project to be easily portable by hand or sent down the telephone lines via a modem.

Information for Manufacturers

The work of the manufacturer is greatly aided if CAD is used at the design stage.

This is simply because the quality and detail of a CAD drawing is far superior to that of a manual drawing. For instance, guaranteed accuracy and drawings that can be provided at any scale reduces the errors and subsequent redesigns that were once an accepted part of the process. The result is a considerable reduction of the design-to-manufacture time.

Another way in which CAD technology has improved the lot of the manufacturer is in using CAD directly to "drive" their machines. That is, computer-aided manufacture (CAM). Many companies use some form of CAM and will quite likely be able to utilize the CAD database to generate the final product.

Information for Clients

As CAD becomes widely accepted throughout all fields of industry, the client increasingly requires more than a pile of drawings at the conclusion of a project. It is becoming commonplace for clients to request the final product in the form of the CAD database, possibly on a series of disks or tapes.

The reasons for the rising popularity of CAD among clients are not just the same as those listed in this chapter. CAD data may be required by companies that do not do design work themselves. The fact is that, to all sorts of people, the database is more useful than a paper drawing. It can be plotted out if desired, many times, but it can also be used in other areas of business such as costing and analysis procedures.

Freedom from Traditional Drawing Office Demarcations

CAD's versatility and adaptability allow its presence to be felt way beyond that of drafting. This has meant the design company changing from what was once a production line of specialist roles—design conception, development, drafting, modeling, costing, liaisoning with manufacturers, and so on—in favor of "creatives" that can take their idea and stick with it throughout the whole project.

As understanding of CAD has progressed from the still too common assumption that CAD is nothing more than an electronic drawing board, its broader scope of possibilities are now being exploited. This inevitably results in the design process returning from the hands of a collection of departments to the individual designer. This empowerment is noticeable throughout each chapter of this book.

Improved Staff Morale

Introducing CAD into the workplace will undoubtedly boost enthusiasm among design staff. The reason for this is simple: for all the reasons stated in this list of capabilities, designers regard CAD as the best tool for the job.

Even those still restricted to manual methods will see CAD as something to aspire toward, some way in which they can develop their talents and careers further.

Staff motivation is important in any business and CAD can play a large part in bringing it about. See Chapter 12 for a more in-depth discussion of staff motivation.

Greater Creative Opportunities

CAD frees the designer from the limitations of pencil and paper. Ideas and concepts can be investigated in an instant. The designer is now allowed to do things that would, previously, have been impossible.

An example of this occurs in three-dimensional CAD work. A complex mesh can be created to display an unusual structure, such as a framework covered by stretched fabric. It is a simple procedure to generate and experiment with numerous designs, each displaying the resulting distortions of the fabric. To even attempt this manually would take an unfeasible amount of calculating and geometry.

Such opportunities allow the designer the creative freedom to take control of and have confidence in her own work.

Broader Project Opportunities

As well as broadening the creative horizons of the individual designer, CAD extends the range of work the designer can attempt. That is, a company once limited to drawing buildings using pen and paper will have the opportunity to tackle a far wider scope of projects with the introduction of CAD techniques.

The versatility of CAD is its greatest attribute. It can be applied anywhere that design is needed, especially when add-on packages are used to augment the basic CAD system.

The design world becomes the CAD designers' oyster. A company's design talents can be employed in fields that would not have been previously considered. For instance, the same system used for architectural design possesses 3D features, and rendering and lighting facilities that can be utilized to design theatre sets.

Marketing Opportunities

The use of CAD in a company often results in positive repercussions in the marketing department (annoyingly not always attributed to CAD).

For example, the simple fact that a company possesses a CAD system may be sufficiently impressive to entice a client to the door. In fact, CAD may pay for itself just by being there when the client comes to visit, whether it is being used or not. (This is a bit depressing, as the reason for discussing all of these capabilities is so that the true worth of CAD can be appreciated, not to con people by making them think that "it looks flashy, so it must be good!")

CAD wins more "pitches." When competing for a job against a number of other companies, CAD gives a pitch that is quick, accurate, and well presented. An impressive presentation can be assembled before the less aware competitors have sharpened their pencils.

Similarly, CAD allows a better response to market needs. Last-minute developments can be incorporated into existing work easily without having to start the presentation process from scratch again.

The transition from "proposal" to "working" drawings is easy, resulting in a short product lead time. Also, the guarantee of accuracy right from the start means that there is little discrepancy in the proposed and actual costs.

The best case a marketing department can present to a client is to say, unequivocally, that their company's work is better than the competitors. "Better" design is, after all, exactly what the client wants. Considering the points raised in this part of the book, it is fair to say that CAD produces "better" designs (although this is controversial to say, especially if you are in a room full of manual designers at the time). Obviously the computer only does what the operator requests, but it is true to say that CAD allows a creative mind to investigate and pursue ideas that would be otherwise impossible. Then, on top of this, there are the advantages such as speed that free the user (designer, architect, engineer, and so on) to pursue their design talent.

Additional CAD Services

A standard CAD package can be applied in a variety of design situations and is not specifically tailored to one in particular. This is certainly true with AutoCAD, the world's best-selling CAD software, which can adapt to almost any design task. A whole industry has developed catering for CAD in these specialist areas.

A design team's creativity can be given a boost by augmenting the basic CAD "engine" by selecting from the host of specialist software and/or add-on packages on offer. This additional software will focus and enhance CAD's capabilities into specific fields of work—architectural, electrical, or surveying, for example.

Specific add-on developments and external services are also available to take completed CAD work and then develop it further. An instance of this is when CAD drawings are used as the setting for a virtual reality scene in which the viewer can interact with the design.

Many bureaus are on hand to provide a wide range of CAD-related services, from the just-given example to more basic tasks such as plotting.

What to Do

Exploit all the benefits that CAD presents:

- Speed
- Neatness
- Accuracy
- Layering
- Viewpoints
- Virtual models
- Reduced external involvement
- Symbol libraries
- Global editing
- Preprogramming
- Intelligent drawings
- Standardization
- Organization
- Quality Control
- Quality Assurance
- Data extraction

- Incorporation of others' CAD data
- Incorporation of previous CAD work
- Interpretation of analysis data
- Numerous output options
- Transferable data
- Data storage and retrieval
- Information for manufacturers
- Information for clients
- Freedom from traditional drawing office demarcations
- Improved staff morale
- Greater creative opportunities
- Broader project opportunities
- Marketing opportunities
- Additional CAD service

4

Building on Initial Enthusiasm

The initial force that often needs to be exerted to bring CAD into a company translates into a momentum afterwards that can assist further progress toward achieving the goals discussed in the previous chapter.

However, it is surprising how soon this momentum can cease, bringing the whole CAD strategy to a halt.

In this chapter, I look at what might cause this to happen and what can be done to ensure that a constant and coherent CAD policy is maintained.

A Bad Start

The successful purchase and installation of a CAD facility is an art that is not in the scope of this book, which assumes an already installed, suitable CAD system. In fact, that subject could warrant a whole book dedicated to it alone.

The reason for introducing CAD is the same as that for any business decision: to satisfy the needs of the company. Prior to implementation, there should, therefore, be a period of research into what those needs are and how well they can best be satisfied by the various CAD set-ups that are available. This task may be performed by a multidisciplinary group from the company reporting to the board.

Failure to approach the implementation process properly is likely to result in a system being installed that does not do what it is required to do. That is, it may be terrific, but not terrific at what it needs to be terrific with in that particular circumstance.

For example, an architectural practice may be impressed by a state-of-the-art system that produces magnificent three-dimensional, photo-realistic images of buildings. But if these images are, in fact, artistic handiwork created with a graphics package, then they are more akin to paintings than engineering drawings. So an architectural practice, where precision is more important than artistic interpretation, would not find this impressive system very useful and would be more suited to an engineering-based CAD package.

The large initial costs of CAD means that, once committed to a specific arrangement, a company can probably not afford to scrap it and try again. Hence, the undesirable situation occurs where staff are having to perform their work using an unsuitable tool, with the obvious consequences.

Initial Assertive Policy

As project experience grows and CAD users become more proficient, the company is enhanced. However, during the difficult initial stages, there are a broad range of measures that should be taken to assure CAD's position in the company.

Exploit any interest shown in CAD by a designer

Install any enthusiastic designer by the CAD facility and offer him all possible help and assistance. They could be an advert to sell the idea of CAD to the remaining and more wary designers. This person can demonstrate to all sectors of the company the practical uses and benefits of CAD that had previously only been talked about in theoretical terms.

Hold CAD designers in high esteem

As interest spreads and usage increases, foster the belief that the CAD designers are taking the opportunity to improve their standing in the company. Treat them with a respect and privilege that sets them above the common or garden manual designers. Arrange for higher levels of pay to be awarded to those possessing CAD skills. This will emphasize that CAD is the way forward for any designer.

Implement training

Training will increase interest, knowledge, and awareness of CAD, and is the key to any company's CAD strategy. Part 5 covers this in detail.

Set minimum levels of CAD expertise for new designers

As new designers are employed, it is important that they possess a CAD capability. No more employ a designer unable to use CAD as a secretary that cannot handle a word processor. The board could issue a directive stating that all newly employed staff must possess a minimum level of CAD expertise. This measure would result in the CAD Manager being involved in the recruitment of all design staff.

Give CAD a high profile

The mystique of the technology must be broken down. Ensure that the CAD system is very visible in the office and provide demonstrations at every opportunity. Advertise exciting new CAD developments in memos circulated throughout the company.

Involve CAD right at a project's start

Any pitch for new work should contain an appropriate CAD element. The people whose job it is to prepare written proposals will have little CAD knowledge, so the personal intervention of the CAD Manager will be necessary to explain what the CAD facility can bring to every piece of potential work.

Provide nonstop CAD justification

Promoting and explaining CAD's capabilities to the whole company is vital to prevent the initial interest and enthusiasm from dying away. This is discussed in more detail in the following section.

CAD Propaganda

The staff member who initially champions the CAD cause to such a degree that its introduction is considered by the board is a leading contender for the role of CAD Manager.

With that success under her belt, the newly appointed CAD Manager thinks that it will be such a smash hit that she need only pause to say "I told you so" and collect a fat pay raise before planning further triumphs. Unfortunately, this is not the way it works, and we all know what pride comes before.

The initial CAD propaganda battle must not be treated as a battle won but rather as an ongoing fact of life. Many a CAD champion, buoyed up by the company's initial enthusiasm, has floundered once this enthusiasm dissipates. When this happens the CAD set-up is in great danger of being relegated to a token gesture of the company's technological commitment. Viewed by the senior management as last year's experiment, it can soon become merely a gimmick to be wheeled out whenever a prospective client visits.

A CAD system is just an expensive pile of electronics. The true value only becomes apparent when it is appropriately integrated into the company's working practices. The benefits that can be reaped and how they can be achieved may seem perfectly clear to you, but nothing will come about unless all sectors of the company are equally sure of and enthusiastic about CAD.

Chapter 3 listed the capabilities constituting CAD's advantages over manual design techniques. These capabilities provide ammunition with which to justify CAD to others. Informing, explaining, and demonstrating these capabilities at every opportunity will reinforce CAD's position as well as bring about the improved utilization of the system.

Such a constant flow of positive views is important to keep the attitude of every member of the company tuned to the same wavelength as the CAD Manager. Any pause in this bombardment and a company's CAD strategy can fail. A constant flow of propaganda, especially in the early stages of a company's CAD investment, can be thought of as an inoculation against weakening enthusiasm (see Fig. 4-1).

Identifying what points to include in the propaganda is not a clear-cut exercise and often varies according to personal viewpoint, the specific CAD set-up within a company, and the field of work in which CAD is being applied.

Personal viewpoint takes effect when different people can see CAD either in a favorable, or not so favorable, light. For instance, showing one person what you believe to be a "neat and clearly presented" CAD drawing may appear "soulless and bland" to them.

The specific CAD set-up within a company is there to deal with their own particular circumstances. These may differ from the "core" benefits as described in Chapter 3.

Figure 4-1. Propaganda will reinforce CAD's position.

The field of work in which CAD is applied can, in a similar way, mean that these core benefits take on different meanings to different people.

It is wise to adapt and tailor the propaganda to specific people or departments that you are speaking with—the finance director, designers, drafters, project managers, senior management, and so on. Each CAD capability provides a springboard from which one can launch into a more detailed and targeted discussion that will help every committed pencil-aided designer to broaden their horizons.

A word of warning: When using propaganda to promote CAD in your workplace, do not get carried away and mislead people, giving the impression that CAD is a magical panacea. This is an easy trap to fall into. For instance, you will regret claiming that CAD will cause productivity to rise like a rocket. It is likely that production will actually fall during the initial period after implementation. Even afterwards, the time-saving advantage of CAD is not apparent when creating new images from scratch, because they occur in the later stages of the design process.

What to Do

- Ensure that the capabilities of your CAD system match its intended purpose.
- Build on any interest shown in CAD by a manual designer.
- Hold CAD designers in high esteem.
- Implement a policy for training.
- Set minimum levels of CAD expertise for new design staff.
- Give CAD a high profile in the company.
- Involve CAD right at the start of a project.
- Provide nonstop CAD justification to all sectors of the business.

5

Overcoming
Negative Attitudes

Once a company has decided to go down the CAD path, it is important that everyone in that company is equally keen to move in the same direction. No matter how worthwhile CAD is in theory, it will get nowhere in practice if the workforce has to be (metaphorically speaking) dragged kicking and screaming against its will to the CAD terminal.

Similarly, it is difficult for designers to make the most of the CAD opportunity if they are troubled by nagging doubts and fears about the technology—whether from inside their own minds or from others in the office.

This chapter covers what makes some workers less than enthusiastic about CAD and how their doubts can be allayed.

The Source of Resentment

People, as a rule, do not welcome change. This is particularly true when the change involves modern technology encroaching on working methods that have served satisfactorily for many years.

This, of course, is exactly what is happening in the drawing office. The drawing board, pencil, and the rest of the draftsman's paraphernalia are being replaced by computers, plotters, and the technological peripherals that accompany CAD. That isn't all: the drawing office possesses an almost mythical reputation for camaraderie with witty banter emanating from behind every drawing board. CAD will disrupt this cozy environment, changing the whole feel of the drawing office as well as the working process.

An initial degree of resentment is, therefore, understandable. The hapless CAD Manager will encounter this negative attitude at all levels within the company, from senior management through to Project

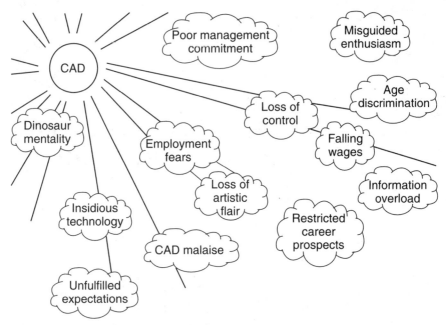

Figure 5-1. Every silver lining has a cloud.

Managers and onto the "shop floor." Individually these doubts may seem minor, but, if ignored, they can combine and grow until they overshadow the reality of the issue (see Fig. 5-1).

This is a matter of concern for many reasons, not the least being its detrimental effects on staff motivation. This important area of successful management is discussed later in the book. Furthermore, any display of resentment, such as a reluctance to accept the introduction of CAD, is resistance to a managerial decision. This is a poor state of affairs as there is no truly satisfactory solution to such a level of resentment.

The complaints arising from the introduction of CAD can be placed under two headings: technical and human. Both are equally important, but the latter is particularly vital to address as these problems are too frequently ignored. The result of this would be the limited success, possibly leading to the complete failure of a company's CAD strategy.

Specific Reasons and Solutions

Here are some common causes of negative attitudes, plus some advice on what can be done to quell these feelings before they have the opportunity to surface.

Notice how obvious they seem and consider how rarely they are tackled effectively.

Poor management commitment

It is infuriating that, although the CAD facility provides the ideal environment for most projects to be tackled, Project Managers are often reluctant to commit their work fully to it. Even if they do utilize the CAD facility, it is often just to provide drafting support for drawing board designers. It is a common paradox that a designer, once given the best design tool (CAD), will not be required to design.

Implementing a more forceful, pro-CAD management policy can combat this negativity. This requires the CAD Manager to have at least the same (and preferably greater) seniority as the Project Managers. Alternatively, a partnership between the CAD Manager and a Director can be formed. Then all projects can be "ordered" onto CAD unless a signed directive from this senior person or partnership decrees otherwise. This method will go a long way toward bridging the "reluctance gap" between Project Managers and the CAD department.

In parallel with this approach, it is important that the CAD Manager knows of new work and pitches at the outset. This is necessary to enable liaison with Project Managers and their teams to advise on CAD involvement in the work ahead. If the CAD Manager is not involved at preliminary meetings, this input will be lacking and the "manual lobby" will win the day, more out of familiarity than superiority.

Loss of control

For years, the whole company structure, from designer to director, has been happy and familiar with the method of production. So when the opportunity is there to work with a CAD system, there is often a reluctance to simply abandon the familiar methods. While agreeing wholeheartedly about the undeniable advantages of CAD, most people have little enthusiasm for putting these words into practice when it comes to work for which they are responsible.

The reason for this reluctance is the fear that the new technology will take away the control they previously enjoyed using manual methods. The control they have worked hard to develop, and subsequently their standing in the company, will appear jeopardized by a new method of production that they are unfamiliar with and know nothing about.

The solution to this problem is two-pronged: a combination of organized training sessions to promote awareness and shouting CAD's praises at every opportunity. The latter should amount to nothing less than a verbal and written onslaught of CAD benefits.

Both solutions should be adapted and directed to individual targets by referring to that person's specific requirements. Then, to give an example, once the senior designer of a "retail floor planning" project is familiar with the sheer bliss of applying CAD techniques to his particular field, he will be converted and shudder at the memories of how he once worked.

By doing this, understanding and familiarity will increase and the acceptance of CAD as a natural part of the design process will subsequently come about.

Loss of artistic flair

One of the chief complaints heard from designers is that, compared to drawing board design, CAD work is impassive. They believe that there is no room for artistic license, feeling, or flair. For all its benefits, they believe that trying to be creative with CAD is like trying to swim with an overcoat on.

This is not so. The advent of CAD in the drawing office should not be viewed as a coup by a ruthless bunch of technos, hell-bent on seeing the manual drafters suffer. No one is suggesting that all pencils and paper should be burned.

The opportunity still exists to sketch initial ideas out by hand. In fact, CAD technology can assist this manual creative process by providing backdrops for the sketches, particularly when complex views (such as perspectives) are involved.

As designers become more proficient in CAD techniques, they will discover the enormous scope for experimentation. This allows ideas to be tried that would never be possible using manual methods. For instance, assessing the repercussions on a design as size and shape are modified is a quick and simple matter using a computer.

Unfulfilled expectations of the technology

Although everyone may be aware that the computer can do great things, there will be times when it does not seem to do the thing that it is required to do. With certain people, this can be the only encouragement they need to reject the whole thing completely. The root of this problem is twofold: poor implementation and underutilization in the workplace.

Exactly what the CAD system does and does not do must be clearly indicated during implementation. If, after implementation, the system is not performing up to expectations, then it may be that a "square peg" has been bought to fill a "round hole." The best recourse then is to contact the supplier and try to make amends.

Once up and running, a company can never expect to reap the full advantage of their CAD system unless it is fully utilized. Not to do so is like a farmer investing in a combined harvester and then only using it to drive to the local shops once a week. It is a fact that the capabilities most users derive from their CAD systems are a mere drop in the ocean compared to the potential on offer. The scope of benefits are enormous (as shown in the previous chapter). To begin to take advantage of the opportunity requires a forthright and imaginative attitude to be taken toward design technology.

CAD malaise

Within a company, there will always be some staff that will take to CAD immediately and feel perfectly at ease with it. Similarly, there will be others that struggle and are unhappy about the disruption CAD brings to them and the tried and tested traditional working practices to which they are accustomed. This latter group of people perpetuate a negative attitude that grips the whole workforce, causing morale and motivation to decline.

This is not a good situation for a CAD department to be in. However, it is unfair to treat this as a "CAD" problem, as it is not. Teething troubles and disruption are inevitable when any new equipment or procedures are introduced, not just CAD. So, as in all such cases, the most important thing is for management to be aware of the problem, to be on the lookout for the symptoms, and to halt this damaging malaise before it takes hold.

Staff morale is an ongoing issue in any business. This book later covers the whole issue of staff motivation and how the problem of low morale can be alleviated among CAD users.

Insidious technology

In any organization using computers, there is always the fear of the same technology being used by management to secretly monitor the workforce. Some people just think that way: when technology enters the office, something sinister "must" be going on.

The image of "Big Brother" watching every move we make is indeed an off-putting one, although generally inappropriate. It is true that computer technology brings the possibility of close monitoring of users into the office. But, in practice, this mostly manifests itself as an aid to the billing of clients for time spent on projects, not spying on staff.

If management did wish to intrude more closely into the work of an individual it is because of that particular management philosophy. That is, it occurs because they want it to, not simply because of the presence of technology. In other words, managers who want to "spy" will spy no matter what, regardless of the presence of computers.

Paradoxically, CAD actually makes it harder to analyze an individual's work. Tasks are fixed and measurable when staff use manual methods. CAD, however, breaks down job differentiation among the workforce, making task allocation less identifiable. Detailed individual monitoring is, therefore, difficult and not a great deal of use.

Employment fears

Since the days of the Luddites there have been fears that advancing technology will leave mass unemployment in its wake. Those that hold this belief are understandably uneasy about the introduction of computers to "do their job," as they see it. There are a few points they are overlooking, however.

For one, CAD is not a robot but a tool used by people. Designers have always used aids to increase their efficiency and effectiveness, and CAD is just another one for them to use.

The move from manual design to CAD will enhance business prospects. This can only result in extra work and hence, extra employment. So, rather than reducing staff, the benefits of CAD often improve staffing prospects.

In the longer term, it is a fact that companies facing the modern world with a realistic understanding of the use of technology are likely to fare better than those not doing so. Those that ignore design technology may well go to the wall losing all jobs, while their clients move to the companies with the CAD capability. Put simply, there is more future for staff in a successful company than an unsuccessful one, and to be successful a design company must acknowledge CAD.

The introduction of new technology is usually accompanied by extensive retraining programs. This is an opportunity that most staff should welcome. Designers' careers will be enhanced by having the extra "CAD" string attached to their bows.

This optimistic news is borne out by case studies that show that the dreaded mass unemployment has not occurred. However, management can go a long way in allaying fears and mistrust by making their belief in these points clear and guaranteeing job security from the outset.

Falling wages

Nowadays, if someone sits all day at a computer, she could be doing virtually anything, from monitoring the company accounts to checking the operation of a satellite.

However, certain misinformed management consider any work done while sitting at a computer to be mindless typing. The fear of some staff is that computing will consequently be considered unskilled work and wages set accordingly.

Thankfully, this frightening ignorance is rapidly disappearing from the boardrooms and, although it exists to some degree, its effect is not as harmful as one might think.

It appears from studies that this fear is misplaced because there is no clear evidence of deteriorating pay levels. In fact, developing CAD skills can improve wage prospects by allowing a designer to stand above the rest. A designer able to use the best design tool (CAD) will enhance their design talent, thus increasing their value in the eyes of an employer.

Restricted career prospects

In the same vein as the previous point, there is a fear that a talented designer will be reduced to a simple computer operator by acquiring CAD skills. That is, rather than it having a positive effect on one's career, it will stifle opportunity and lead to a career dead-end.

Sadly, this is a quite justifiable fear. Designers with CAD skills, possessing abilities beyond many of their contemporaries, find themselves used as supporting staff to the less able manual designers. This is an absurd waste of resources.

It does not have to be like this. As long as management is aware of this dangerous pitfall, CAD can give careers a new lease on life. Often this will mean a sideways as well as a forwards step. While many designers master a powerful new tool, improving their design abilities, others shift their job specification completely.

Since the introduction of CAD, there are a whole range of responsibilities to be taken care of, some of which can merge with existing design duties and others like "CAD Trainer" that can be full-time duties.

Information overload

A member of staff transferring from manual to computer methods of design is likely to experience the feeling of being swamped by information. That is, the increased possibilities presented by the technology and the speed of activity result in the user being overwhelmed. This constant state of anxiety will lead to stress.

This is a very common symptom in people encountering unfamiliar new technology. The problem will arise whenever staff are moving from a situation in which they control the pace of work to one where the computer seems to control the pace.

The degree to which people are affected varies greatly. To many, this massive increase in information is an opportunity, not a problem. It is a matter of individual attitude whether it causes stress or not.

The only real solution is the awareness and understanding of the management. Communicating an appreciation of the problem and explaining the cause in terms similar to those mentioned here will go a long way to diffusing any anxiety. The alternative is for the feelings of stress and inability to cope to dominate, resulting in consequences that are detrimental to all concerned.

Age discrimination

"I'm too old" is a frequently heard refrain when CAD is mentioned, as if it were something for the "young'uns" to play on—like a skateboard—rather than a tool for anyone seriously involved in design.

Contrary to what many believe, age has nothing to do with CAD ability, although it is true that there are differences in the way age groups perceive and come to grips with technology. For instance, the older staff members, more set in their manual ways, tend to ask more questions and want to see evidence of CAD's benefits.

The CAD Manager and anyone training these people must be aware of this. Obviously they are skeptical about abandoning their perfectly acceptable methods to go back to square one with an experiment in modern technology. Proof must be provided to displace the years of evidence they possess supporting the traditional approach.

The argument for using CAD technology in particular must be made, rather than expecting the need to keep up with technology to be a sufficient argument for the move to CAD.

The reticence of the older members of staff may partly be due to the fear of appearing ignorant in front of the younger and more computer-literate staff. This is unnecessary, since the skills of the manual designer (architect, engineer, and so on) are still respected and needed in the CAD world. All these people need is an additional CAD ability. They have nothing to fear from computer whiz kids who have mastered that single talent but are beginners when it comes to design experience.

Dinosaur mentality

In addition to the characters already mentioned in this discussion on negative attitudes, there are more troublesome individuals to contend with. Dinosaurs still roam the design offices of the world and their ignorance, shortsightedness, and small-mindedness cannot be underestimated.

Even when the CAD system is up, running, and proving its worth, this element of the workforce is likely to contribute to the proceedings with such comments as, "We managed perfectly well without CAD" or, "I could have drawn that quicker on a drawing board." These are quotes from endangered species. They make such comments to try to drag CAD's progression back and prolong their own existence.

These people are not just a bit bewildered, in need of help and support, but they also have their heads planted firmly in the sand (a dinosaur relation of the ostrich?) and have no intention of removing them. They do not even pretend to be enthusiastic about the theory of CAD—never mind putting it into practice.

Clarifying to them what seems as clear as day to us is the biggest task that CAD Management presents.

Misguided enthusiasm

This is not so much a negative attitude as a harmful positive attitude. For some, the temptation to use every possible command overwhelms their desire to perform the work they have been set. The designer may be more interested in exploring the new CAD world than in designing.

Even when keeping their minds on the task at hand, they may waste time by, for instance, using the zoom facility to work on a complex detail that will not even be visible when the drawing is finally plotted.

This may spread to nondesign activity. An introduction to computer technology can turn someone into a "hacker" overnight. The mere knowledge of a password restriction will seem like a challenge, and they will dedicate as much time as possible to finding it out.

This problem's solution is to harness the enthusiasm. For example, assign this person with a task to create a customized menu for a symbol library. Make sure that they only use these talents when told, and only on assigned projects. Such work can be offered as treats: "If you concentrate and finish up your work, I'll have a bit of programming for you to do."

What to Do

- Have a clear pro-CAD company policy.
- Give the CAD Manager sufficient authority to carry out the policy.
- Involve the CAD Manager in the project's planning from the outset.
- Provide "CAD awareness" training for all who need it.
- Preach the CAD philosophy to the whole workforce.
- Allow traditional design techniques to complement CAD methods.
- Use a CAD set-up appropriate for the job.
- Exploit all of CAD's capabilities.
- Halt any malaise and motivate staff.
- Embrace CAD and improve career prospects.
- Preempt stress from technology-related pressures.
- Exploit wisdom gained from experience in manual design projects in CAD projects.
- Tackle any influences that may be detrimental to the success of the CAD office.
- Develop new careers created by the CAD working practice.
- Exploit talents that become apparent as staff become CAD-literate.

Implementation

Simply replacing drawing boards with computers is inappropriate: they are different things that have different functions.

The new role played by CAD in the company needs to be clearly identified. For instance, should it be considered a fully integrated part of the design process, or should it be treated as a detached facility that provides a bureau service to the rest of the company?

Next, decisions must be made regarding the extent of the range of equipment, the reach of the data throughout the organization, and the working conditions conducive to modern design methods.

This part of the book investigates how these strategic decisions can dramatically help or hinder the success of a company's CAD initiative.

6

The Role of the CAD Department

Attempts to exploit the potential capabilities of CAD are likely to be ineffective unless the role that CAD is to play in the company is clearly defined and understood by everyone.

"What role—don't you just get it out of the box and plug it in?" Well, no. If you do that, CAD will be used like a new toy, whereas if you define its role in the company, it can be put to work.

There are two distinct alternatives:

- A CAD bureau within the company, with dedicated computer terminals operated by CAD specialists, providing a service to the designers.

- A fully integrated policy where the CAD facility is a tool used by designers as an integral part of their day-to-day activity.

This chapter examines the pros and cons of the different approaches.

CAD and Management Philosophy

An expensive CAD system alone does not make an effective CAD strategy. The role of CAD in the company must be carefully considered; otherwise, attempts to achieve the capabilities described in Chapter 3 will be confused and directionless. It is not a technical preference, like choosing which type of computer or operating system to use. Rather it is a matter of management philosophy.

The technique can be an "internal bureau" where designers request work from the CAD department as they would do from an external bureau, or it can be an "integrated design tool" approach incorporating CAD techniques seamlessly into the company's design process. The

	Internal bureau	Integrated design tool
Computers	Designated to CAD work	Designated to a project
Staff	CAD specialists	Designers with CAD skills

Figure 6-1. The application of computers and staff in CAD departments with differing roles.

way in which computers and staff are applied in each case are indicated in Fig. 6-1.

In each case, the computers are the same machines with the same software. The difference occurs in the way they are put to use. A CAD bureau service within a company will require dedicated terminals in the same way that a company library has its own books. A fully integrated approach, however, places CAD directly in the hands of the designer like any other design tool—though a very powerful one.

Who uses the machines—specialist CAD operators or specialist designers with limited CAD skills—largely depends on the work to be done. CAD specialists may be required to translate verbal and sketched instructions into high-quality CAD data. Alternatively, a specialist knowledge of a particular discipline, say architecture or manufacturing techniques, may be needed to tackle the work. Whatever the role of the CAD department, be aware of the danger of employing the wrong "type" of CAD designer.

Once the role of the CAD department has been identified, it should be made clear to everyone concerned. It is possible to have both roles functioning simultaneously—again, as long as that is understood by everyone. The important thing is that the whole workforce is aware of and playing by the same rules.

When one person's view of the role played by CAD is not compatible with another's, conflict can occur. For instance, resentment will build up if designers working with a fully integrated CAD system find themselves under pressure to perform CAD chores for other designers in the company.

In practice, company policy tends to float somewhere between the two extremes of the bureau and the integrated approach. Each brings its own potential pitfalls. Combining them, however, is more likely to produce a wider range of pitfalls than a happy compromise.

The most suitable function of the CAD department depends on particular business requirements. Generally speaking, I have found a favorable solution to be as described under the "integrated design tool" approach but with the additional contribution of CAD specialists. They are necessary to enable designers to exploit the potential of CAD. Their absence may mean designers remaining ignorant about valuable techniques and possibilities.

The Internal Bureau

Though the fully integrated method is surely the way of the future, not all companies have the equipment and appropriate staff to commit fully to that policy now.

Consider a company employing 200 people. If they purchase only three CAD terminals, they cannot possibly throw out all of their drawing boards and attempt to become fully computerized. This situation usually means a CAD bureau policy will be followed, possibly with full integration as the eventual objective.

With the bureau approach, the creative process lies predominantly with manual methods. Designs created either on paper or just in the minds of manual designers are recreated using CAD methods. Any feedback on the design goes to the manual designer who will make revisions and hand it back to the CAD bureau to update the CAD file. This is a design equivalent of the typing pool and, as shown in Fig. 6-2, brings with it problems of poor communication and motivation.

The CAD specialists who carry out the work exhibit a greater eagerness to develop their skills and experiment to get the maximum advantage from the tools available than a "run of the mill" CAD-able designer. This has a positive effect causing the utilization of CAD in the company to improve and expand.

For this same reason, sit one CAD specialist next to another, and the whole becomes greater than the sum of the two components. That is, work is enhanced by the mutual enabling that inevitably takes place.

Operating a CAD bureau approach has many benefits, though it still has drawbacks. For instance, talented designers, encouraged to attain

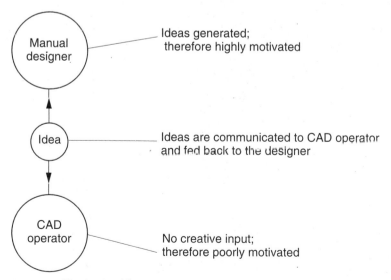

Figure 6-2. The internal bureau.

CAD skills, can find their valuable talents only succeed in moving them from a designing role to a drafting role in the CAD bureau. A paradox occurs whereby skill levels increase, yet there is a net reduction in the effectiveness of the workforce.

The Integrated Design Tool

The bureau approach tends to attract basic drafting work that far from exploits CAD's potential, whereas an integrated facility allows designers to explore and then develop their own ideas (see Fig. 6-3). Because of this, when CAD plays an integral part in a company's design process, it's likely to be utilized as the complete design tool that it is.

Gradually, more designers who have been raised on CAD are coming into the workplace—inevitably encouraging the shift toward full integration. The stumbling blocks of poor communication and reduced enthusiasm, present whenever a CAD operator has to interpret the wishes of a manual designer, are being eroded as the terms designer and CAD specialist become synonymous.

Even when committed to integration, the company must choose between grouping machines together or having one per desk throughout the building. The strategic and the physical pros and cons of grouping or dispersing CAD terminals are dealt with in the following chapter. One big advantage of integrating the CAD facility throughout the office is that the project management tasks are kept in the hands of the Project Manager (where they should be), rather than falling to the CAD Manager (as they often are if the work is carried out in his department).

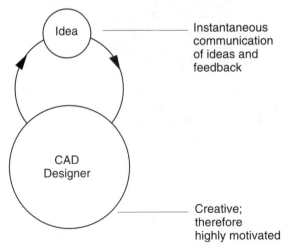

Figure 6-3. The integrated design tool.

There are drawbacks, however. The CAD Manager may consider it a triumph to gain the board's backing to get CAD machines placed throughout the workplace, one for every lucky designer. However, if the creative staff do not view the function of CAD in the same positive way, cajoling unwilling designers onto CAD by replacing their drawing boards with computers is only likely to damage morale and stifle creativity.

What to Do

- Assess the work to be done and allocate CAD staff and computers appropriately.
- Apply them according to a well-defined role. This may be a "bureau" approach, a "fully integrated" approach, or somewhere in between.
- Ensure that this role is understood and adhered to by the whole workforce.

7

The Working Environment

A tremendous advantage can be gained from an appropriate working environment, both for the individual designer using the CAD facility and for the company as a whole applying the investment strategically. It is an area comprising two issues; the siting of the CAD facility and the conditions conducive for work.

Siting CAD

What are the pros and cons of siting CAD users and their equipment either in a separate area designated specially for them or alongside other designers working on the same project, wherever that may be in the building?

Why location matters

In the previous chapter, CAD's function within the company was discussed. Whether an internal bureau, full integration, or somewhere in between is chosen, there is a further strategic decision to be made. Are those that use CAD to be grouped according to their discipline — CAD — or according to their team, with fellow project workers?

Discipline-based implies that an area of the building is allocated for all the CAD equipment and users. A designated CAD location clearly suits the internal bureau approach very well. However, there is no reason why an integrated approach should preclude grouping according to discipline. True, the machines are not exactly at the designers' fingertips, especially in larger organizations, where the physical separation may be very inconvenient. But practical considerations may mean that grouping CAD equipment is the cheaper, simpler, and possibly the only option.

Team-based location means that when a project involves CAD, the CAD operator will work alongside others in the project, wherever that may be in the building. This is not necessarily the dream scheme of one per desk, but it is integration of CAD with the design process. Whether the operators are designers or CAD specialists is a different matter. Even if CAD specialists are involved, they are clearly associated with that team's project and are not available for general exploitation. Consequently, team-based CAD tends to preclude the internal bureau approach.

In the real world, of course, we are dictated to by events just as much as we dictate events. Even with an established integrated system, a degree of CAD terminal clustering will inevitably take place as practical restrictions (such as cabling) take effect.

A company introducing 1 or 2 CAD terminals into the business will find a clustered approach is the simplest way to get up and running. As time passes and the system develops, the decision must be made between grouping or dispersing the machines. The company's management should direct events accordingly. A "let's just see what happens" approach will lead to problems, frustration, and unfulfilled expectations.

The pros of grouping tend to be the cons of dispersal and vice versa, and both options will be considered individually.

Discipline-based

Grouping equipment and people into a designated area shouldn't suggest an isolated environment. Placing everything and everybody related to CAD into a separate room with minimal contact with the outside world is like putting an eagle in a bird cage: such a degree of isolation inhibits the characteristics that made it so appealing in the first place.

A discipline-based CAD department should be sited in the same area of the building as the rest of the design activity in order to prevent the CAD department from becoming detached and (ultimately) irrelevant to the design process. Grouping it in the center of the action will allow CAD to play its rightful role as the kingpin in design projects.

Locate it here, among the designers, but clustered together and detached from the drawing boards, so as to discourage the monopolization of a machine by any one designer.

Here are some advantages of a discipline-based CAD department.

Marketing The prestige value of CAD is such that its simple presence in an office can be sufficient to win over a prospective client. It is wise to exploit this advantage and locate it in a highly visible dedicated area. Focusing attention on this positive image, rather than less advanced areas of the business, can bring in customers before the system has even been put to use!

Flexibility Placing all resources in a single area allows greater freedom within the CAD group. That is, flexibility is possible among users and equipment, enabling resources to be easily reallocated to cope with periods of uneven workloads.

Interaction Grouping together workstations will allow interaction to take place that results in the dissemination of knowledge among users. Similarly, having all resources in one area has obvious advantages for training.

System management A CAD Manager needs to be able to oversee her CAD "empire"—facilitated by the increased accessibility clustering brings about.

This is particularly important in that only one set of security procedures needs to be implemented in a designated area, and that the CAD Manager is easily accessible, in the place where he is needed most. Other benefits include maintenance, general system management, the implementation of standardization procedures, and the monitoring of output—all greatly enhanced by grouping the department.

Environmental The conditions necessary for CAD work—discussed in detail later in this chapter—can be satisfied more fully by creating a single, ideal environment for a number of machines rather than by creating many little ones for each machine throughout the building. Practical problems, such as linking to a plotter or to a backup device, are obviously simplified when all equipment is gathered together.

Should the CAD system need to be moved, either to a different part of the building or to a different building altogether, localized cabling allows the CAD department to be "picked up" and moved as a single whole unit.

Team-based

The term "team-based" describes a situation where CAD is located according to project requirements—usually alongside the rest of the design team.

If you are reading this and you work in a small one-room organization employing less than 10 people, you will be understandably saying to yourself, "What's the difference? 'Discipline-based' means that I sit here with the CAD machine, and 'team-based' means I sit here with the CAD machine." In this situation, the difference is more in attitude than location. The contrast is more apparent in larger organizations, where, say, in a 5-story building employing 100 potential users, the choice is between CAD machines grouped in one corner of the building or sited (as telephones are) where they are needed.

Here are some of the advantages of dispersing the CAD system to the project teams.

Integration The biggest advantage of placing a CAD machine with the project team that needs it is the instant integration of CAD into the design process. CAD becomes part of the company rather than an alien presence, detached from the world of design and designers.

Linking CAD equipment so visibly to a project will discourage the thought that CAD is a service facility like a photocopier, for general exploitation.

Locating the CAD designer with other designers involved in the same project makes all the relevant reference material and data easily accessible. Similarly, the rest of the project team can benefit from easy access to the CAD facility.

Staffing More appropriate staff will be employed if they are brought in to build the project team rather than to augment the CAD department. For instance, a Project Manager may choose a suitably qualified CAD designer, where the CAD Manager would have mistakenly taken on a less suitable general CAD operator.

Siting It is possible to "hardwire" a whole building so that computer points will be as accessible as electricity sockets. Simply plug a CAD terminal into the nearest point and a connection is made to the network and plotter.

A well-installed hardwired system gives freedom within a building, though it cannot be taken with you if you move to a different building.

Working Conditions

Working conditions have a dramatic effect on the worker and (subsequently) the work being done. Considerate planning involves common business sense and an understanding of health matters. Specific solutions can be applied to such areas as seating layout, equipment layout, plotters, storage, cable layout, and lighting.

Why working conditions matter

After examining the role that the CAD system can fulfill in a company (Chapter 6) and the significance of the facility's location (previous section), we now turn our attention to the working conditions necessary for the successful application of CAD.

Creating a suitable working environment is not normally a pressing concern for senior management. However, when long hours are being spent at a computer terminal, the working environment dramatically effects the worker and subsequently the work being done.

Initially one would think that CAD was a relatively harmless occupation, especially when compared to heavy industry, mining, or the factory floor, but it does have its own particular problems. For instance, a computer screen looks harmless compared to a gigantic, noisy, dirty mechanical machine, but it is the cause of much concern about health. As the problem of screen radiation has been largely overcome, the display is still a prime cause of discomfort due to glare, image flicker, poor readability, image brightness, and inappropriate workstation design—all of which generate aches, pains, and stress throughout the body. In the extreme, it may mean staff unable to work at their CAD terminal after relatively short periods of time.

Frequently, the root of the problem is found when CAD is introduced into a design office as a replacement for drawing boards. This can lead to the CAD system being laid out in exactly the same way as the drawing boards were. This is a mistake, as CAD is not the same as drawing boards and pencils: they are completely different things, and each requires particular environmental considerations. For a start, CAD will require more space, especially when plotters, media, and laying-out space are taken into account.

The failure of management to understand CAD working conditions can result in an operator being presented with the bits and pieces of a CAD system plonked on a wobbly table with a bar stool to sit on. Consider the CAD designer at work. There are computer displays (often two) to be constantly monitored, a hand-operated mouse and a mouse-operated digitizer, plus paper drawings and notes to be frequently referred to. All of these elements need to be accounted for; otherwise, the unfortunate CAD operator will suffer fatigue and discomfort that could have been easily avoided by the adequate provision of acceptable working conditions.

Planning working conditions involves taking into account common business sense and health care.

Common business sense dictates that an appropriate working environment will raise job satisfaction among the workforce, and as their attitude to work improves, productivity will rise correspondingly.

Awareness of health issues has increased as computer use has spread throughout business. However, it is still alarmingly common for a worker to suffer great discomfort unnecessarily on a daily basis without the true cause being identified. The medical and legal professions are divided over the implications of these so-called "repetitive strain injuries." In Europe, companies are being guided by a directive on minimum health and safety standards which comes into force in 1996.

Specific solutions

Solving the problem of poor working conditions is not a subject for debate but is a problem with objective solutions and tangible benefits. It is simply not worth putting up with inferior standards when the following common sense proposals are so easy to implement.

Seating layout The optimum set-up consists of an adjustable swivel chair, providing good back support, and a U-shaped desk designed with sufficient legroom to allow swiveling. Second choice would be the L-shaped desk, with the poor old single desk, bowed and creaking under the strain, coming last.

Drawer space should be incorporated to provide a "private space" for the user and to prevent a cluttered work surface.

Space, possibly a shelf, must be available for the numerous manuals that need to be in easy reach during work sessions.

Equipment layout Unlike the average word processor—which is light, compact, and simple—CAD equipment is heavy, cumbersome, and comes in many bits and pieces (increasing in number as technological developments produce more and more useful gizmos).

Because of this inflexibility, thought must be given to positioning the equipment to avoid the harm that will otherwise become apparent.

From the tips of your fingers to the top of your head, you are susceptible to Repetitive Strain Injury (RSI). This can be partly solved by sensible workload planning. But, it can be greatly alleviated by the considerate positioning of equipment (see Fig. 7-1).

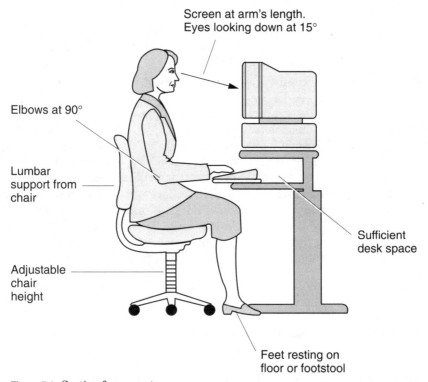

Figure 7-1. Seating for computer use.

For instance, a seemingly simple matter such as positioning the screen warrants careful consideration. It should be positioned so as to avoid any reflections. This might be accomplished using techniques such as those mentioned later under "Lighting." The height of the screen determines the angle of the user's head while she looks at it. Putting it on top of the main computer case may make it too high, and not doing so may make it too low. Either situation is unsatisfactory. An upright spine and neck with the eyes looking out at approximately 90 degrees is preferable. The screen must be sensibly incorporated with the rest of the equipment; in other words, it's no good to not be able to see the screen while using the keyboard. An often-forgotten matter is the user's handedness—left or right. The relationship between screen and other equipment, such as the tablet menu, will differ accordingly.

Plotters Plotters vary tremendously in size and type. Nevertheless, there are certain general points to bear in mind when siting them in an office.

Laser plotters are larger and heavier than their pen plotter counterparts, but they are much quieter. Electrostatic plotters, which are in between the others as far as weight and noise are concerned, use dielectric paper, which creates "cut-off" wastage that will swamp any busy drawing office.

Ideally, plotters are best isolated, though still near the computers, as even the quieter ones are irritating after a while.

All electronic equipment, especially certain plotters, create a lot of heat, causing discomfort to anyone in the room. Suitable cooling and ventilation should therefore be available to counteract any overheating.

Plotting media comes with guidelines on temperature requirements and general care. Presuming the office conditions are suitable it is best to keep paper near the plotter for easy access. As a rough guide to suitable conditions, a temperature of between 18 and 24 degrees Celsius, with suitable air circulation from either natural sources or air conditioning, is desirable.

Storage Do not forget the need for storing drawings after plotting. You may have a system where completed work is whisked away to another department immediately. Chances are, however, that drawings will accumulate. A storage device (such as a plan chest) is advisable.

As well as the storage of the various media, additional storage will be required for backup and archive material, though this may be in a different part of the building, such as a secure room or safe.

Cable layout It is amazing how easily cabling can get into such a confused mess. Apart from unsightliness, there is the danger of the plug accidentally being pulled at an inopportune moment and the difficulty in adding or removing particular pieces of equipment from the system.

Do not underestimate the amount of cabling required, and how frequently cables will need to be removed and replaced. Specific cabling depends on whether the machines are separate, networked, or clustered around a shared plotter. There may be special power requirements—numerous power points that need to be grouped and/or movable. Additional telephone points will be needed if modems are used. These things must be considered to avoid not only a mess but dangerous and crash-prone cabling.

Matters can be clarified with a cable identification system, perhaps using colors and numbers. Cables that may otherwise be too close to feet could be neatly hidden away above a suspended ceiling, below flooring, or behind wall partitions and trunking.

Lighting Inappropriate lighting is a common cause of eye strain, headaches, and nausea. Though only temporary conditions, these things are unpleasant and severely impair the work being carried out.

Numerous ways exist to reduce detrimental effects of poor lighting. Positioning users' backs to the wall is a big help, as it reduces screen glare dramatically. Fluorescent lights can be "neutralized" by fitting them with diffusers. Dimmer switches put brightness control in the hands of those working in the room. Using desk lamps rather than room lighting is an even better solution; then lighting can be positioned to illuminate only where it is needed. Sunlight entering through windows can be blocked by blinds and curtains.

A range of anti-glare filter screens can be attached to any computer screen to reduce glare. (First, however, get a demonstration in your workplace before purchasing them, as they are not the panacea they may at first seem.)

Regular eye test entitlement and the provision of glasses if needed should be provided (by law) for computer operators. Eye tests can often detect a problem caused by working conditions before the worker is even aware of it.

While on the health issue, one of the most worthwhile things a manager can do when tackling these matters is to consult the workforce. They will say exactly what inhibits their ability to carry out their work.

Health information and training must be available to staff. Their working practices must include provision for getting away from the screen, either to attend to other work or get out for a break.

What to Do

- Consider the various pros and cons before siting the CAD facility.

- Decide whether the company would be better with a solution that is team-based or discipline-based.

- Ensure that working conditions do not have a detrimental effect on the workforce or their work by considering such things as seating layout, equipment layout, plotters, storage, cable layout, and lighting.

Chapter

8

Broadening CAD's Range

This chapter and the next describe how the boundary of CAD's involvement in a business can be expanded.

This chapter is concerned more with the actual generation of design data, which involves spreading out beyond the core system across the full extent of technological activity. Broadening the range of data generation can be thought of as a "horizontal" development across a company.

Developments beyond the core system will not be looked at from the technician's or reviewer's viewpoint but instead examine the strategic and managerial implications of any such action.

Three primary routes can extend the range of a company's CAD system: networks, modems, and data transfer. These are not the only options available, but most others include aspects of at least one of these three. For example, Computer-Aided Manufacture (CAM) allows CAD design data to be utilized in product manufacturing. It may involve taking CAD data from a network, translating it into a format intelligible to the CAM system, then transmitting it to the manufacturer via a modem. Hence, all three routes are involved in extending the scope of CAD's influence.

Networks

Within the confines of an office a Local Area Network (LAN) can be set up using direct links between devices (computers, printers, modems, etc.). Widespread electronic data communication going beyond the office requires a Wide Area Network (WAN). With the advent of the Internet, the telephone system—with its comprehensive access to industry, commerce, public places, and homes—is the basis for future wide area networking.

Why network?

The chief reason behind any networking is to share a common data-base and allow the exchange of data between terminals. The "CAD base" is, therefore, spread without the need for floppy disks and the costs, delays, and limitations this would incur.

As well as the CAD database, peripheral equipment can be shared. Sharing a plotter between many users is a major advance on pushing the plotter around the office, unplugging and plugging in cables and altering T-switches. A networked plotter allows the user to send a plot with minimal effort and disruption. Similarly, other equipment, such as a modem, added to the system immediately becomes accessible to the whole network (see Fig. 8-1).

Another big time and disruption saver is the ability to perform operations from one point rather than visiting each terminal individually. For instance, the data from each terminal can be backed up in a single action.

Practical concerns

The interconnecting cable needs to be more than just a piece of coaxial and connectors. The length and fragility of the cable and the number

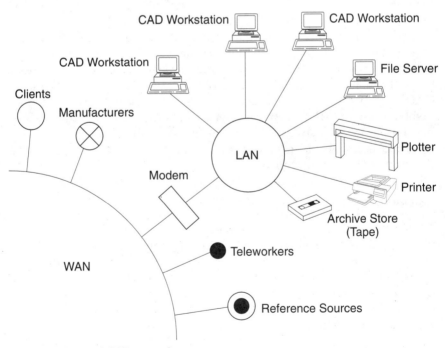

Figure 8-1. A typical CAD network.

of connections to be made to it must be considered when planning a network.

There will be times when one needs to disconnect a machine without disrupting the whole network. Therefore, it is wise to use connectors that do not break the circuit when they are unplugged. Preferably, with large networks, spread over a wide area, look into ways of isolating certain areas. Sometimes this can be accomplished with software that includes an "error threshold" which, when passed, causes the automatic isolation of the problem terminal.

Cabling problems can be reduced by removing the visible cabling and "hardwiring" the building. Terminals are then simply plugged in wherever they are wanted throughout the building.

A network extends the generation of CAD data. This, therefore, raises the possibility of a data "jam" occurring in the system. This is a technical problem that involves allocating files and memory availability to the right places. Preempting this problem allows it to be easily dealt with by the supplier

On the subject of the supplier, before any network is installed the CAD Manager must make sure that all queries and requests have been answered satisfactorily.

Here are four common questions regarding a general network:

- What is the limit to the number of machines on the network?
- Can it be expanded if necessary?
- Can it be linked to other systems?
- If one machine "crashes" does the whole network go down with it?

It is worth getting the answers in writing to prevent dissatisfaction later on.

Visiting an existing working example of the network you are interested in and speaking to unbiased users of the system goes a long way to allaying fears and identifying problems that you might not have considered. Any reputable supplier will be happy to arrange such a visit; if they aren't, be suspicious.

Network management

Networking produces new system management tasks that are often taken on by the CAD Manager. However, management of a large and complex network can be a sizeable role that could be allocated as a job in its own right. The tasks of the Network Manager, whoever it may be, fall into four categories:

- Configuration of equipment running on a network is more complex than that of a stand-alone machine. There are many files and procedures that only someone possessing a specialist knowledge would be familiar with. Consequently, many CAD Managers need training, while others delegate the tasks and some organize a telephone hot-line support run by an expert. Whatever you do, keep a backup of all configuration files and regularly check memory usage.

■ Operational effectiveness does not remain fixed at a constant level, as many assume. Numerous users performing various tasks, making different links across the network, makes the system appear like a single, gigantic, complex machine. Consequently, it needs to be fine-tuned to produce its best results. In other words, increasing a memory allocation may produce the equivalent results of (say) a corresponding increase in the engine capacity of a car.

■ Fault recovery must be quick and allow only minimal damage to occur. Besides emergency measures, preventative action must be taken as well. For instance, a problem can be resolved while set procedures—such as the regular backing up of work—ensure that only a small amount of work is lost. A good network will include some degree of in-built fault management allowing it to diagnose problems, and sometimes before they even occur.

■ Security leads the manager into the world of passwords, access, and data protection (covered later in Chapter 18). It must be possible for a person with the right password to access relevant data while having access to restricted information blocked.

Modems

A modem converts digital data into a series of audible tones that are transmitted via the telephone system to another modem which reverses the process to recreate the digital data. Figure 8-2 demonstrates this process. So, something, in this case a CAD database, can be "beamed up," like on *Star Trek,* from one computer, travel across the world in the form of a telephone "message," and then rematerialize on a different computer.

Why modem?

The opportunities a modem presents are widespread. It extends the range of a computer in the same way that a telephone extends the range of our personal communication.

A very practical use of the modem is to improve support arrangements. A modem link allows instant access to your computer files by a specialist who, if necessary, can download data directly from his office computer.

In fact, all dealings with those outside the office can be accomplished quicker and easier. Work can be communicated to freelancers

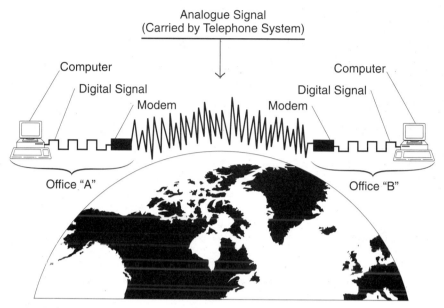

Figure 8-2. The transmission of data via modem.

or bureaus during busy times. Files can be sent for plotting to bureaus. Sending work out for external procedures, such as converting to 35mm slide format or to a lithographer for model construction, are simplified.

A modem will improve client liaisons, allowing work to flow back and forth, at any time of day or night. Similarly, communication with the manufacturer will be enhanced.

Also, there are additional uses that are increasing all the time, such as access to bulletin boards and the sending and receiving of electronic mail (e-mail).

A modem link can transform the working practices of a company. It is quite feasible for staff to work at home on a computer linked to the central office computer. This would be more applicable to some industries than others.

"Teleworking" is becoming increasingly popular as it frees companies of many overhead costs and offers the staff flexibility. It is especially popular with those who are unable to work the normal 9-to-5 routine, such as those with young children or disabilities. Where large amounts of data are involved, the potentially lengthy and expensive calls can be reduced using data compression techniques.

Practical concerns

The key practical question when installing a modem is "Is this modem suitable for what I want it to do?" Firstly, the modem must be able to perform the tasks required of it, and, secondly, it must be applicable to the particular work situation.

Technical information on the specifications of modems is readily available from suppliers. However, here are three basic points to consider when purchasing a modem:

- *The interface:* Is it suited to your work situation?
- *The commands:* Are there clear, user-friendly commands and an on-line help facility?
- *The transfer process:* How good is it at recovering from a crash? Is file compression automatic? Are progress and results of a transmission indicated on screen?

Data Transfer

In this chapter, data transfer refers to the transfer of data between dissimilar formats — that is, the translation of data from one computer format to another.

Why transfer data?

Transfer may take place across departments in a company or outside the company to a client (for example). In each case, a gap is being bridged, allowing CAD techniques to be effective over a wider area. The link may be made to other CAD systems, DTP systems, and differing types of computer.

Having an open pathway between your company's CAD system and, say, that of a client, is not only useful but is often a prerequisite of many clients that will stipulate a compatible CAD system before they will even consider signing a contract.

Several hundred CAD systems exist today, as well as the swarm of DTP and graphics packages, all sharing some common ground but each possessing many idiosyncrasies. Consequently, data transfer is rarely a straightforward process. A procedure for transferring data from one format to another is only successful until its weaknesses are discovered. Some may fail at the text font hurdle, others at line thickness, and — for those that survive these initial obstacles — there are further pitfalls ahead, 3-dimensional data being a common source of distress.

Data transfer techniques can be applied to the following situations.

Between dissimilar CAD systems

This could be achieved by scanning or digitizing one system's CAD drawings onto another's. The actual CAD data is most suitable, preferably via a "direct" transfer. However, considering the number of CAD systems available, this may not be possible. Transferring to a "neutral" format is more practical.

A generally applicable neutral format is the intermediate filetype. Figure 8-3 shows a representation of how CAD data can be converted to a filetype that is acceptable to other systems. Once accepted by a second CAD system, the file will be translated into the CAD drawing, allowing full access and editing rights.

With the AutoCAD software package there are two well-used intermediate filetypes—DXF and IGES—although both are far from ideal. The recent development of the STEP method for data transfer (the STandard for Exchange of Product data) is the latest attempt to rationalize the procedure. This has been developed as an ISO standard and will probably supersede DXF and IGES.

Unfortunately the intermediate filetype procedure is not always free of problems. Usually a transfer does take place, but with bits of information lost in the process. The reason for this is usually that the

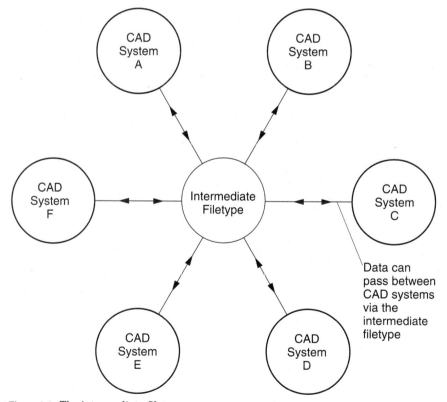

Figure 8-3. The intermediate filetype.

CAD data being sent comprises sophisticated entities that the receiving system cannot support — 3-dimensional drawing elements, for instance. Or, there may be differing system configurations: different values set for decimal place accuracy, the maximum number of Layers, segments in a Polyline, and so on.

Between CAD and DTP systems

There has been a proliferation in recent years of software under the desktop publishing banner. Their common feature is that they all manipulate text and graphics. Bridging the gap between CAD and DTP broadens CAD's base tremendously, adding a more "polished," presentational aspect to CAD work. The ability to enhance the generation of design drawings to include text manipulation can lead to the almost simultaneous production of product manuals and other things.

Most DTP systems accept CAD plotfiles as well as DXFs, though color and line thickness will often be lost. Once in the DTP system the CAD image can be manipulated with the various DTP tools that can spruce up a CAD drawing to make it more presentable.

Between IBM and MAC systems

This is a different ballgame. As well as the numerous CAD packages for IBM-compatible machines, there are a plethora of CAD, graphic, and DTP packages available for Macintosh computers.

Any situation involving exchanges between IBM and MAC systems should be treated individually. Suppliers and their ilk will tell you how any IBM CAD drawing can be zapped into QuarkXpress on the MAC as easy as D.X.F. But the truth emerges when your CAD drawing contains anything other than the most basic entities. Try it with 3-D work or drawings including AutoCAD's paper/model space combinations, for example; then the process is not so successful.

So treat each transfer route individually rather than relying on one rule for all. There is nearly always a way through the transfer maze; it may involve hunting down specific translation software, or using an intermediate step (such as converting 3-D CAD to 2-D CAD) before translation.

When testing a translation process, you should use a specially created drawing that includes everything: 2D, 3D, text, fonts, colors, blocks, polylines, viewports, Paper Space, Model Space, and whatever else you can think of!

What to Do

Networks

- Choose the networking system that suits your needs.
- Increase access to all CAD equipment with a LAN.
- Extend the access and the range of CAD data beyond the office with a WAN.
- Ensure that the network is managed appropriately.

Modems

- Choose a modem system that is relevant to your needs.
- Connect your CAD system to the telephone system and exploit its worldwide network. Use modems to improve access for support arrangements, external facilities, client liaison, data for manufacturers, bulletin boards, e-mail, teleworking, etc.

Data transfer

- Transfer data between dissimilar CAD systems to, for example, extend access to clients' CAD data.
- Transfer data between CAD and DTP systems to, for example, create quality manuals.
- Transfer CAD data between IBM and MAC systems to extend into a massive sector of the design world.

Chapter

9

Exploiting CAD Throughout the Business

Since the arrival in the design office of the personal CAD system the productivity of the individual designer has risen like a rocket. Paradoxically, however, the productivity of the company as a whole has not always displayed such a dramatic increase.

The likely reason for this is that, too frequently, the companywide exploitation of the opportunity afforded by CAD is prevented from progressing beyond first base. CAD is providing the designer with a better drafting tool than a drawing board and pencil, but that's all. Whichever route is followed regarding the function of the department, and no matter how much investment is made in equipment to extend CAD's range, it is a fact that the rewards from investing in CAD will be severely limited if it is used as nothing more than an electronic drawing board.

Previous chapters have shown how the CAD database can be extended "horizontally"; this chapter will show how to exploit the database "vertically" throughout the business.

For this kind of integration to take place, CAD data must not be viewed in isolation but made accessible and allowed to benefit other areas throughout the whole design to manufacture process.

Increasing the reach of CAD is possible and desirable, whatever the internal structure of a company. Allowing every department access to the product data will produce effects as rewarding for the company as those experienced by the individual designer.

Time-consuming repetition, conversion, and updating of work as it passes from one department to the next will be eliminated. Response time to changes in design will be reduced, and the single entry of data will give fewer initial errors. As well as these obvious benefits, more indirect advantages will appear, such as improved interdepartmental relationships.

Two terms often used by CAD suppliers, dealers, and so on, are *drawing management* and *data management*. Frequently these are used interchangeably and incorrectly. The former refers to the management of information within the confines of a particular CAD system. The latter, however, is on a much larger scale; independent from the CAD system, it goes beyond to integrate with other areas of a business. This will be discussed first.

Accessing CAD Data

The reduction in cost and size of CAD machines combined with their increasing power has resulted in their becoming commonplace in today's office. The days have passed when CAD meant an expensive bulky piece of machinery that had to be shared by a number of people.

It is also true, unfortunately, that CAD systems are not as user-friendly as they could be. With word processors, most people (and even occasional users) can figure out how to create a document. Yet, CAD's complexity places it out of bounds for a majority of people. This need not be a problem though, as utilizing information from the database does not necessarily require CAD knowledge, and when access to CAD drawn files is necessary, customized interfaces can simplify the task.

To maximize access to CAD data, specially designed software is required to link the company's various systems together and filter out the relevant information for each department. This is equivalent to selecting the appropriate implement from the multipurpose tool, shown in Fig. 9-1. The managers, the engineers, the marketing team, the accounts department, and many others will be able to utilize and build on the information that they access.

The extent to which databases can be exploited is obviously greater if all the departments in the company are computerized. For instance, the Windows OLE (object linking and embedding) capability allows data developed in different departments with other Windows applications to be joined into a single piece of work. The example shown in Fig. 9-2 shows spreadsheets and bitmaps incorporated into a drawing created with AutoCAD Release 13.

The benefits derived from CAD have been examined in Chapter 3; this section shows how CAD's benefits are not restricted to the CAD department but are commonly available to all departments.

Who Can Benefit from CAD Data?

Unlike a paper drawing, which is one thing and one thing only—a paper drawing—CAD data is a vast collection of images and statistics

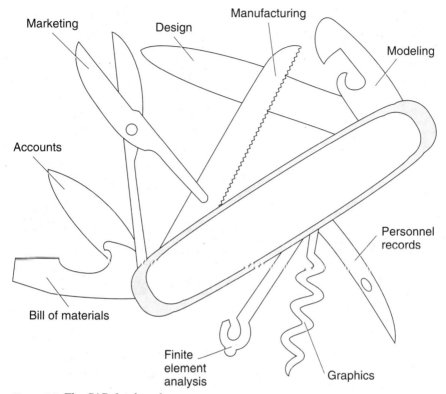

Figure 9-1. The CAD database has many uses.

related to the design. So, who else can use this data once the CAD user
has finished with it (or even if they haven't)?

General design staff

Even just among the (non-CAD) design staff, partial access will allow
them to view CAD-generated drawings as well as the facts and figures
that accompany them.

Images extracted from a CAD "drawing" can include details, parts
and assembly drawings, prototypes, symbols, and standardized items.
The statistical content may be a drawing register, parts lists, a bill of
materials, and time sheets.

Imagine, for example, architects and all the various people and
departments that they deal with all accessing the same database. This
would facilitate communication and strengthen their working relationships. Not only that, it would encourage the coherent and efficient
development of a project.

A single piece of the CAD database may be utilized by more than one
person or department. For instance, a drawing office manager may

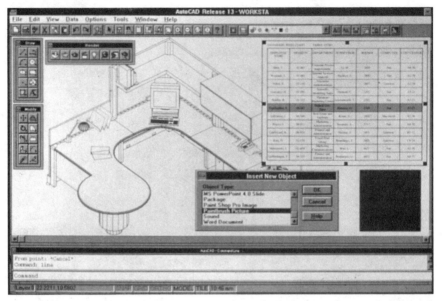

Figure 9-2. The incorporation of external data with a CAD drawing. *(Autodesk Ltd.)*

monitor progress with the help of the data from the computer-generated drawing register, while the client account manager may access the same data to aid their liaison with the client.

Rather than just handing paper plots of drawings to the graphics department, they can access the data themselves. If all they require is a paper plot then they can plot the drawing, but if they want more, then they have that opportunity. For instance, having access to the specifications of a complex curved surface held in the CAD database will save the person designing graphics to fit that surface a lot of time and effort.

Similarly, in-house or external model makers will benefit from the detailed knowledge of the product that the database can impart. At its most basic, printouts at 1:1 scale provide a template from which to trace. In some cases, the "model" is created on the computer (discussed under the following heading).

Direct access to all CAD data is a clear boon to the specification writers and anyone involved in the preparation of manuals documenting the work being done. Statistics can be retrieved on any aspect of the project, whether it be the bill of materials or the number of tiles to be used, from a single source—the CAD database.

Having information on-line regarding the time each user has spent on a project, what work has been issued, and when it was issued makes for quick and extremely effective financial management of projects.

Computerized accounts packages tied in with the CAD network make accessible at the push of a button what would previously have required searching through acres of paperwork.

Of course, a computerized store of information on all the company's design projects being available at one's fingertips makes a valuable in-house reference library. Not only that, such readily accessible information would be welcomed by senior management wishing to keep abreast of activity.

Engineering and manufacturing

Many of today's working practices incur the simultaneous accessibility of information. For instance, "concurrent engineering," where many aspects of a project are tackled in parallel rather than sequentially, would not be possible without up-to-date information from the CAD database being easily available to design, manufacturing, sales departments, and others.

Nowadays the design to manufacture process is likely to be computer-aided from start to finish—that is, CAD to CAM (computer-aided manufacture). As a result of these modern working methods it is possible to, among other things, minimize lead times, raw material stocks, and the time spent making the product. The CAD to CAM process is present in a range of disciplines, from construction to fashion. It involves not just two stages, CAD and CAM, but many phases and alternative routes to follow.

To start with, the basic CAD drawing can be improved to provide a 3-dimensional image. This may involve solid modeling—computer-generated images that can be likened to a model cut out of solid material—or surface modeling—computer-generated images that can be likened to the skin that covers the 3-dimensional object.

Then there are the possibilities brought about by specialist calculations, such as parametric design, automatic part listing, and finite element analysis. Engineering analysis has benefited from computerization for some time. It is only relatively recently, however, that the computational representation of a CAD drawing has been convertible into a form compatible with the requirements of analysis methods. This allows the two to be directly linked. Now it is possible to run finite element analysis software within the CAD drawing itself.

The prototyping stage in the process can be costly and time-consuming, though undeniably necessary. The objective of prototyping is to identify problems before committing to the real thing. For example, there may be problems in the manufacturing, assembly, or ergonomics of the product.

Many of these problems can be identified on-screen using 3-dimensional modeling. Where an actual physical model is still necessary, rapid prototyping is available. There are a number of different approaches to rapid prototyping to meet the variety of products being designed. Most build on the procedure used to convert CAD data into 2-dimensional pen movements on a plotter. A common and successful method uses laser beams to fuse together powder into a solid mass. Similarly, stereolithography uses laser beams to solidify epoxy resin.

Finally, we get to the point where something is actually going to be manufactured. Using the CAD file as CAM input data allows the operator to initially simulate the cutting procedure on a computer. Tools and tool path can be selected, tried out, and then, when the operator is satisfied with the outcome, the computer simulation data is sent to the actual machine and the product is cut.

Marketing

As CAD is becoming commonplace any company that does not move with the customer and respond to their needs is going to lose that customer to a company that can. The benefits of CAD to a company's marketing strategy are enormous.

When pitching for new work CAD allows quicker and better proposals to be presented rather than the hastily prepared engineering drawings which, because of their "roughness," will be virtually useless should the pitch succeed. With CAD techniques, a proposal can consist of engineering drawings prepared neater and more accurately than their manual counterparts, and (what's more) from this information it is easy to generate detail close-ups, assembly diagrams, 3-dimensional images, even animation. This level of thoroughness and accuracy provides a usable basis from which to work on the project proper.

The ability to experiment and test a prototype on-screen, minimize errors, estimate accurately costs and materials, and do many other things allows us to accurately say that CAD results in better designs — which is the best marketing there is.

What to Do

Utilize CAD data for:

- Drawing records
- Costing
- Engineering analysis
- Marketing
- Manufacturing
- Accounts
- Specification writers
- Model-making

4

Staff

Matching the right person to the job is a problem encountered in any business, but particularly in the uncharted territory of new technology.

As mentioned many times throughout this book, CAD is not an electronic drawing board but a complete design solution. Similarly, a computer-aided designer is not necessarily the same person as a manual designer. The creative and productive freedom of CAD may be too much for a traditional drafter to cope with. Of course, they may embrace the opportunity that CAD has presented them with, finally allowing them to leave the drafting chores behind and concentrate on designing.

If new staff are recruited, what talents should they possess: design skills, CAD operating skills, computer skills? In fact, how can they be recruited if the employer is still firmly rooted in traditional working methods?

The talented designer who gains CAD skills may, paradoxically, find himself at a career dead-end. Unless the company can exploit these talents, such a designer can find himself simply inputting information on behalf of drawing board designers.

The three chapters contained in this part of the book deal with these issues. They can be summed up as follows:

- *What makes an ideal CAD user?*
- *How do you recruit them?*
- *Once you have got them, how do you keep them?*

10

The Ideal CAD User

The subject of personnel is a broad one and not one to be discussed here extensively. This book is concerned with the success of the CAD investment and so will here examine the particular qualities of the successful CAD user. Many of these qualities also apply to other employees, some not even involved with CAD, so this text will be valuable to any employee — or at least those involved with creative technology.

Because of the rapidly changing nature of CAD technology, some managers may worry that bringing in talented newcomers will only highlight their own weaknesses. This is a misguided approach. As any good manager knows, employing people that are "weaker" individuals than yourself will only result in a weaker whole. To build a strong, dynamic, and successful empire "strong" people are needed (see Fig.10-1). Employing staff with the qualities mentioned in this chapter will allow the department (and then the company) to grow and develop.

This is true generally, but particularly so in the area of CAD. There are plenty of CAD operators looking for work, but to achieve the benefits listed in Chapter 3 of this book, users with certain qualities are essential. Without such staff, there will be little chance of realizing the full potential of the CAD investment.

As well as these qualities, always required in CAD staff, additional skills related to a company's particular field of work will be requested by an employer. The ideal CAD user will have the following traits.

Ability

There is a prerequisite level of competency that any self-respecting CAD user should be able to meet. As software and hardware become more and more powerful, so expectations rise. Not many years ago simply being able to use CAD techniques at all would have been

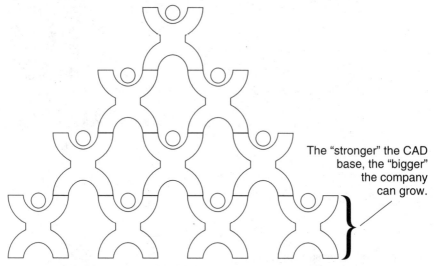

The "stronger" the CAD base, the "bigger" the company can grow.

Figure 10-1. Employing talented CAD staff will strengthen the whole company.

considered impressive. Now that these techniques are commonplace, it takes a greater demonstration of ability to gain praise.

Job security, especially in the design industry, is virtually a thing of the past. However, ability will always be in demand, so prospective job candidates must be eager to stay up-to-date and ahead of the competition in their field.

The obvious way to improve one's ability is through training, and this is covered elsewhere in this book in great detail.

Many people who have recently learned the basics of CAD will discover that it does not necessarily mean that they will be able to cope with the more complex tasks faced in the workplace. Being able to adapt to these circumstances is a measure of true ability and is not as commonplace as some users would have their employers believe.

Experience

CAD experience should be broad-based and include knowledge of subjects surrounding any specialist areas, which can then be a foundation for gaining further experience. For instance, an experienced user will be at ease with the design technology and sufficiently familiar with basic operating system commands to implement file management and so on.

As CAD usage has such enormous scope, a very experienced designer may appear inept because the experience does not cover the area relevant to the job. That is where expertise comes in.

Expertise

A specialist knowledge of the field of work is an important requirement. Management unfamiliar with CAD have been known to employ staff simply because they use CAD techniques. If it had been a drawing board designer they required, they would never have dreamed of just employing someone because they had good drawing skills; they would be concerned with skills in the area relevant to that particular job.

Well, the same applies to CAD. A brilliant CAD operator with vast understanding of the field of Printed Circuit Board design would not be a good choice for an interior design project.

Receptivity

The ability and willingness to build on past experience and gain more, possibly through training, is very valuable. However, not everyone is receptive to change, nor does everyone want to be

In the rapidly developing field of creative technology, it is essential that the person using it is willing and able to perceive new developments and different ways of applying them.

Enthusiasm

People attending a job interview almost always appear enthusiastic. The difficult thing is differentiating between those who will maintain this enthusiasm after the interview has finished from those who will not.

Enthusiasm and experience make a valuable combination, but do not confuse one with the other. Someone may be able to talk confidently about 3-dimensional rendering, for example, but it may be with the enthusiasm of a person wishing to learn more about it rather than a person already proficient.

That is not to say that experience always wins over enthusiasm. If a company is prepared to train new staff, then an enthusiastic candidate would be a better investment than one with more talent but no desire to learn.

Inquisitiveness

The "naturals" usually learn their skill in the first place by being inquisitive and exploring the new world CAD has presented them with. They explore options, are not afraid to experiment, and use commands in unusual ways to achieve the result they want.

A way of identifying this characteristic in staff is to observe their readiness to refer to their CAD manuals to look for new and alternative techniques. The sort of employee who does this will make a positive contribution to a business. Those who don't tend to lack the positive and inquiring attitude needed to optimize the opportunity CAD presents.

Responsibility

What was said under the previous heading is not intended to encourage a maverick approach to work; a level of responsibility must also be maintained. A good inquisitive person will also know when it is time not to experiment. Some employers may want to play safe altogether and employ someone not so inquiring, so as to simply get on with the work without attempting to improve methods or outcome. This is counterproductive, though, as an innovative and inquiring mind will drive the work forward, while lack of such initiative could actually be a liability. It is true, though, that occasionally you may require a "robot"—but even then, a "robot" with some spirit and intelligence is preferable to a complete automaton.

During everyday work, a CAD user must bear the responsibility for identifying and avoiding errors where possible. There may also be the added requirement of performing tasks laid out by company procedures (including Quality Assurance documentation, for example).

The trust that a company manager must have in the CAD staff occurs when she feels that the employees are responsible. If irresponsible staff are employed, they might still learn responsibility but only from the mistakes they make at that company.

Motivation

Although design work is usually team-based, the individual designer must be able to pursue his own work without constant assistance from others.

Also, the CAD user must be aware that the work will undoubtedly involve periods of dull, repetitive work, as well as times for initiative and experimentation. A mature and conscientious attitude is required to tackle the day-to-day mundane periods of CAD work. The operator must be able to stick with a task until it is completed.

Motivation of staff can be encouraged when the circumstances detailed in Chapter 12 are present in the workplace. However, the individual should not expect the company to do the motivating. It is a matter of personal attitude before anything else.

Creativity

The benefits of a creative person will extend throughout the whole of a business. They will not only find original solutions to CAD problems, but will suggest imaginative applications for the CAD system. This person will exploit the CAD system's range and the CAD data's reach throughout the company.

A word of warning: the person whose interest flits about in the wider scheme of things rather than actually getting the work done on time is not so good. These people are not so much creative but simply lack focus in their approach to work.

What to Do

A CAD staff should possess the following traits:

- Technical ability
- Broad-based CAD experience
- Expertise in a relevant field
- Receptivity to new developments
- Enthusiasm for CAD and the work
- An inquisitive attitude toward CAD
- Responsible working methods
- Personal motivation
- A creative and innovative mind

11

Recruitment and Assessment

As we approach the end of the twentieth century, figures for unemployment that would once have been unthinkable are now considered acceptable. Whether we are experiencing a boom or a slump, there are always plenty of people looking for work, and, more than likely, there will be at least one of them who is perfectly suited to a company's needs. Someone who will appear tailor-made to fit the requirements of the position. The tricky thing, however, is to bring perfect candidate and company together.

This chapter covers the whole recruitment and assessment process. This subject can be viewed from two perspectives: employer and employee. Whichever way you look at it, the subject is the same; consequently, this chapter will be of equal value to both interested parties. For the sake of clarity, however, the information will be directed toward the employer, although the employee can gain from it as well.

Searching for Staff

There are three primary recruitment routes to explore: advertisements, employment agencies, and personal contacts.

Employment agencies

At first glance, these seem like the perfect solution — an organization that links company and candidate like a personnel switchboard. However, in reality, no agency has every employee and employer on their books, but only a tiny fraction of them.

Do not despair, though; many employment agencies specialize in a particular area. Depending on the vacancy, an agency could be chosen that deals in, say, design, computing, or CAD. This narrows the field somewhat.

In most cases, the employer pays the agency's fees. Fees are usually fixed, so the cost is known at the outset — unlike advertising, which might need to be repeated many times before the right person is found. Costs can be high, often the equivalent of the employee's wages for a couple of months or so, although deals can always be done for regular clients.

The only worthwhile agencies are those that can be relied upon to screen all applicants according to the specifications given to them and then send the company only the most appropriate people from which they can make the final choice.

Advertisements

Job vacancies may be advertised in:

- *National newspapers:* Relatively expensive, large audience.
- *Local newspapers:* Less expensive, smaller audience.
- *Magazines and journals:* Varied cost, targeted audience.

In each case, the standard procedure is to place an advertisement that clearly describes the requirements of the position, request a resumé with covering letter, then filter out candidates for interview from the responses, after which the successful applicant is hopefully found.

This method is cheaper in the short run than employment agencies, but it requires much more time and effort on the part of the employer to find the right person.

If the vacancy is for a person with a specific expertise (3-dimensional CAD and rendering skills, for instance), then an advertisement in *CAD User* magazine would give better results than one placed in *The Times*.

Personal contacts

In my experience, word of mouth is one of the most successful methods of finding suitable employees. A bank of "contacts" covering a variety of skills in the field of computer-aided design can be accomplished intentionally or allowed to accrue naturally over time. Also, every CAD Manager will no doubt have a file full of speculative resumés that regularly arrive in the mail.

From this network of people it may be possible to find Mr. or Ms. Right. If not, pursuing these contacts may well lead to a wider network of similarly talented people from which a suitable person may be found. This is a quick and cheap method of searching for staff.

Permanent, Part-time, Contract, or Freelance?

Nowadays more than ever, there is flexibility in the job market. Both the employer's and employee's desires and expectations have changed. It is no longer expected that a vacancy will be filled by a permanent member of staff, with the employer taking on all the additional responsibilities which that entails until retirement day.

The decision whether to employ permanent, part-time, contract, or freelance staff involves the consideration of these points:

- How much work with CAD potential is coming up and when? Will the number of CAD terminals available and the amount of work to be done result in operators or machines being idle or is there surplus work?

- What is the current staffing situation?

- When do existing freelancers leave and contracts expire?

- Compare the cost of a freelancer or contractor with that of a full-timer, but remember that regular use of freelancers and contractors may incur the cost of employment agencies and advertising.

- There is a cost, in time and money, for the induction period needed every time a new person needs to be familiarized with the system and the work.

- Compare the cost of training a fulltimer in downtime with that of laying off a higher rate freelancer and then reemploying them when needed.

- The constant presence of fulltimers allows them to assist and enable the less CAD-competent.

- A freelancer is usually taken on for one particular project, whereas a fulltimer can take on quick jobs as well as long-term work and "float" between projects.

- The CAD Manager needs to be able to advertise to the rest of the company what can be done with CAD with the knowledge that there is someone there to do it. Not having the staff available will result in unfulfilled promises, which then leads to mistrust of CAD throughout the company.

- Fulltimers will set the standards on backing up, storage, cataloging, Quality Assurance procedures, and so on. Occasional employees would then follow this lead. Keeping to standards would be difficult with occasional employees alone.

- A team of fulltimers creates a feeling of esprit de corps in the department, inducing a strong commitment to their work and to the company.

- Among the CAD staff at any time, there should be a range of capabilities to match the range of work.

- Short-term staffing problems, such as illness and holidays, will always need to be overcome.

On balance, after considering the points just raised, it would seem that permanent staff are nearly always the preferable option. Yet it is a fact that short-term, freelance, and contract staff are becoming more and more commonplace.

This is most likely the result of two overriding reasons.

Firstly, freelance staff are often taken on at very short notice in panicked response to a staff shortfall. Secondly, the short-term costs of freelance staff are low due to employees only paying for that person's productive time. There are no paid holidays, paid days off sick, national insurance contributions, and so on. Over longer periods, though, the cost per hour of a freelancer is difficult to justify unless they are constantly productive and generating income for the company. Recent trends indicate that employers are trying for the best of all worlds by offering staff fixed-term contracts.

Application Forms and Interviews

Once a shortlist of candidates has been arrived at, the application form and then a subsequent interview are used to indicate whether the candidate approaches the standards of the "ideal CAD user," as described in Chapter 10. The application form provides an excellent foundation for the interview. An accompanying handwritten letter may be useful to give the applicant the opportunity to fill in any areas that they feel the form has missed.

A well-thought-out, neat, and clearly presented application form implies that a candidate's drawings will be the same. Does it look as if they have taken their time over it, double-checked it for spelling errors, and so on? Has thought been put into text layout and printing?

Involving the more experienced CAD operators in the selection process may be useful, but beware of two possible problems here. First, the in-house expert may only be a big fish because they are in a small pool. That is, they may not be the know-it-all they seem to be and will be impressed, therefore, by anyone with greater skills. Secondly, your expert may not be very keen to hand over the expert's crown and will be inclined to recommend someone less capable than themselves.

References given on the application form should be followed up. They may reveal crucial information on the candidate's background. For example, someone who has worked at all the best design companies may have done so because they impress at interviews, but once in, are so unpopular that they are dismissed at the first opportunity.

The application form covers the applicant's personal details, qualifications, and experience. The following points are more specific and may be discussed in greater depth at the interview:

- Ask them what they think the job entails. This will highlight anyone with unrealistic job expectations that may be unwilling to tackle the work that is required.

- Ask them to describe previous related work. When they do this, observe their communication skills and see if they display enthusiasm and knowledge. It is up to the interviewer to evaluate whether the candidate is telling the whole truth about their experience or straying from the actuality.

- Ask them how they rate their own CAD skills. This question is not just used to find the person with the greatest CAD talent; more importantly, it uncovers if the applicant has a realistic view of CAD. A beginner who realizes there is a lot to learn and is keen to do so is preferable to a more knowledgeable applicant who thinks that they have learned all there is to know and will not progress.

- Ask how they learned their skills. Were courses taken, or did they teach themselves? Their answer will display their interest in the subject and also indicate how well they perceive new ideas. A person's response to these last two questions will reveal to what extent he has learned, or is learning, the skills necessary to perform the necessary tasks.

- Personal interests may give a clue as to whether the applicant will "fit in." This is more important when interviewing someone for a post in a small, friendly office.

- Do they possess any hidden talents that could be utilized by the company? Often they may be unaware that they have a talent, such as a language, that adds a valuable string to their bow.

- Listen to the candidate speak. If the interviewer does all the talking, she will not hear what the candidate has to say. However, do not let the interviewee "play for time" by rambling, as this will just waste the opportunity.

- Observe body language. This can be used to confirm verbal signals of confidence, for example. Another simple indicator is to note how the interviewer feels after the interview—bored, anxious, positive, etc.

- Look at the candidate's work portfolio. It is preferable to view it on a computer rather than paper. A drawing done using inferior CAD techniques can still appear impressive on paper, but entering into the actual CAD drawing file allows their technique to be evaluated. For instance, look out for such things as intelligent layering.

Practical Appraisal

After the interview, when hopefully both interviewer and interviewee are feeling at ease, it may be worthwhile providing an opportunity for the candidate to demonstrate their skills in a practical session. This will weed out the con-men/women and identify the truly talented, who may not sell themselves as well as they deserve in interview.

The following look at appraisal is written from the employer's point of view but is also intended to give employees an insight into what their prospective employers are looking for.

Hands-on session

Be careful not to put unfair obstacles in the candidate's way. For example, your company may have a customized method of entering the CAD drawing editor and specialist command menus. If these are explained, a reasonably bright person will be able to utilize them; otherwise, even the most talented of CAD experts will not be capable of even starting a drawing.

There is no point in frightening the candidate with a complex drawing that only somebody already working in your company would be able to make sense of. A simple drawing that lets them demonstrate those specific abilities that are required will be sufficient. Also, do not rush them, as it is a test of their skills more than their speed.

While they are drawing, look at more than just the final drawing. Do they use CAD's design aids, set their own text and dimension styles, use "Blocks," "Layers," and so on?

Do they appear familiar with most of the commands? How do they input them? Are they quick, typing in the commands not accessible from the command menus and not needing to read through each set of subcommand options before choosing?

Does the final drawing look neat? The drawing may be correct but some are better presented than others, especially where text and dimensions are concerned.

When completed, further testing can be carried out by requesting specific tasks such as using the "Distance" and "List" commands to inspect parts of the drawing. This can tell you three things:

- the drawing's accuracy
- the candidate's familiarity with these checking commands
- her reaction to having her worked scrutinized

This final point is an important consideration otherwise difficult to discover. If they resent others criticizing their work, they may not be suited to the company's method of working.

Commercially available CAD tests

It is very common for there to be a knowledge and ability gap between the candidate and the interviewer. In some cases, it is a "Grand Canyon."

In such a situation, it can be a good idea to incorporate a "ready-made" CAD test in the candidate's assessment.

Commercially available programs can be purchased for this purpose, usually entailing multiple-choice questions, selected from a large pool held in the computer's memory, to test the scope of the applicants' CAD knowledge. Beware though: these tests can also be purchased by a candidate!

It is not a good idea to rely too heavily on commercially available test programs, at least for the reason that the questions asked may not be applicable to the actual job to be done. Also, they can give misleading results. For example, they may ask a question on a command that a proficient user would deliberately avoid, possibly because it is slow and they have found a more effective way to achieve the same results. A novice, being familiar with the "by the book" method, is more likely to provide the answer desired by the computer program. The hands-on method, described previously, however, would allow the proficient user to be recognized as the better of the two candidates.

What to Do

- Choose the most appropriate recruitment method — employment agencies, advertisements, personal contacts.
- Decide the most suitable terms of employment — permanent, part-time, contract, freelance.
- Give careful thought to the preparation of application forms, as they can tell a lot about how valuable an applicant will be to the CAD team.
- Use interviews for assessment of personal attitude, job expectations, and CAD skills.
- Hands-on sessions or commercially available tests can be used to verify CAD ability.

12

Staff Motivation

Why bother about motivation? Surely staff either do the work or they don't, and if they don't, they go. Simple as that.

Well, no, it's not as simple as that. Motivating staff can mean the difference between an "as-long-as-I-look-like-I'm-doing-something-until-it's-time-to-go-home" mentality and a genuinely concerned and enthusiastic attitude toward the work and the company.

Do not confuse motivation with staff willing to work until they drop. The image of the boss standing at the helm, overseeing the terrified workforce, ready to crack the whip the instant anybody lifts their eyes from the computer terminal, is misguided. In fact this attitude would result in the opposite outcome to that desired, actually demotivating the workforce.

The aim of staff motivation is to create an atmosphere in the company of genuine enthusiasm for the work being done, where every member of staff is aware that they "are" the company. So put down that whip and let's examine the effects of (and the methods for) achieving a positive attitude in the CAD department that will radiate throughout the rest of the company.

The Benefits of Motivation

The repercussions of a well-motivated workforce fall into three broad categories:

Business objectives

A well-motivated workforce possesses a focused and committed attitude to realizing business objectives. They have a sense of direction that means that each individual task is considered a small, yet vital, step in the company's overall journey. The result of a workforce united in their mission is the eventual success of that company. To put it very simply:

$$\text{increased motivation} \rightarrow \text{increased production}$$

Job satisfaction

They may not even be aware of it themselves, but staff that are not motivated will gradually become bored and frustrated with their work. Any initial interest will disappear as job satisfaction and morale slumps. The repercussions are self-perpetuating. Poor morale among the workforce will lead to fundamental problems in the future.

Fortunately, the opposite is also true. A well-motivated workforce possess a positive attitude that raises job satisfaction and makes an effective contribution to the company.

Undeniably important though this is, job satisfaction is intangible. That is, it is not easy to quantify. Having said that, a workforce that is motivated exudes an attitude that has clearly identifiable results. Work is completed on time with fewer errors in a happy atmosphere.

Resource exploitation

The CAD software available today is incredibly powerful, but its potential impact is not always realized. If a company is fortunate enough to have a value facility such as CAD and staff capable of doing great things with it, it is clearly wise to maximize the returns on the investment. This can only be achieved by a workforce that is fully motivated.

If nonmotivation is allowed to result in nonexploited resources, it must be understood that this includes the human resource. Lack of motivation can lead to the departure of key players to competing companies where an interest will be taken in their motivation.

What Motivates Staff?

To create a scenario where the consequences of motivation just described are brought about, it is necessary to know what ingredients and conditions are conducive to its development.

An initial key requirement is for management to recognize the importance of staff motivation and then act in a way that will bring it about. This involves a degree of wisdom and psychology on the part of the management that is too often missing from the younger, inexperienced management found in much of today's design business.

The staff are concerned with their own particular duties and are not in a position to view the CAD department and the company from an overall perspective. This can only really be done by management. The

CAD Manager must exploit their senior position to encourage staff motivation, which will assist the CAD department in becoming a positive force within the company.

The manager of the CAD department should be in the happy position of experiencing the pleasure of heading the department that is at the forefront of developments in the company. Ensure first that this is so and second that the staff is aware of it. This will boost their self-esteem, as well as their standing among their peers.

The actual function of the CAD department and all its member staff must be apparent to everyone concerned. Individual responsibilities should be clarified and the management structure clearly defined, including how the CAD Manager fits into the scheme of things. Staff need to know, for example, whether their role is part of the design team or a detached CAD bureau servicing the whole company.

This issue overlaps with that of Quality Assurance (dealt with in Part 8 of this book). A requirement for QA is a Company Policy document. Within that policy would be the CAD Policy, which should identify who is responsible for what and how work is delegated to the people actually seated at the computers.

Talented staff, willing and able to do great things, must not be restricted by their superiors. For instance, many well-paid and well-respected management continue to treat their staff as if they are telepathic and automatically know exactly what their task is. They are not telepathic and consequently have a frustrating time trying to achieve an aim that has not been made clear to them. There must be communication between management and workforce to alleviate the guesswork and last-minute panics. To this end, staff briefings must be considered a priority—not a nice idea that rarely materializes.

Staff involvement outside their own immediate tasks should be encouraged, for example, by delegating the opportunity to attend conferences and exhibitions, and then reporting back to the rest of the department. As well as freeing some of the manager's time and providing useful material, it also generates the feeling of being a valued member of the team able to contribute to the overall effort.

The biggest boost to motivation occurs when staff are "developing" rather than stagnating. This does not mean bullying tactics, nor does it advocate regular promotions for everyone. Staff must be helped to grow "within the scope of their particular job specification."

Therefore, a lull in the workload can be utilized as a time for staff development. It is hardly motivating to know that, after having committed time and effort to finishing a project, you will simply be laid off.

The most obvious method of developing staff is training (see Part 5 of this book). It makes good sense to nurture and encourage those that impressed with their willingness to learn during their initial interviews by providing the opportunity to train in one way or another. This may only involve the decision to move them near to an experienced CAD designer. A simple act like that can turn them from being stagnant and frustrated to dynamic and enthusiastic as they seize the chance to develop their skills.

Measures such as this allow interest to flourish among staff, whatever their level of experience. Just the opportunity to discuss and share information among fellow CAD designers will reduce tension and dissatisfaction, as well as improve CAD skills.

Internal user meetings, chaired by the CAD Manager, can be used as a focal point for discussions among workers. Progress, problems, wishes, and suggestions can all be aired and acted upon. Occasionally including outsiders, such as a representative from a support company, can make a useful contribution.

Too often, rather than gaining CAD expertise being recognized as an attribute, it can bring a person's career progression to a halt. The talented member of staff is restricted to being an "operator," while less-talented contemporaries bypass them by following the traditional career route. This is a common cause of staff irritation. The best designers deserve to be allowed to design with the best design tools (CAD).

As more people become proficient in CAD, others will be compelled to follow suit and the standing of the CAD department will grow from strength to strength. The mere presence of an aficionado in a CAD group will inspire and motivate. Even by example alone, this person will provide the impetus for enthusiasm in CAD and a desire for greater achievement in the department.

Smoothing out the link between designer and CAD terminal can have a massive impact on the work done. For instance, by considering the "user-friendliness" of new software purchases, or by customizing existing software, day-to-day problems and delays will be bypassed. This type of action will have the additional consequence of reducing the time needed for training.

There are many obstacles that can hinder a person's work, and a major one is the working environment (see Chapter 7). The Board of Directors may have committed large sums of money to a CAD investment, yet are only reaping a fraction of the potential rewards by not considering working conditions. The effect on staff motivation is undeniable. Imagine the effect on your motivation if you knew on your way into work that the glare caused by the position of the computer screen will cause a headache before 11 A.M.

"That's all very well," you may say, "but that all becomes irrelevant when the prime motivator is mentioned — money." Surprisingly, pay is not usually considered by the workforce to be as important as job satisfaction. In fact, successful staff motivation will create a tolerance to a company's financial situation. In other words, money cannot buy staff motivation. A big pay packet will attract new employees and encourage existing ones to stay, but staff morale and motivation will suffer unless the issues discussed in this chapter are taken into account.

What to Do

- Recognize the issue of staff motivation and deal with it from the top of the company.
- Clarify everyone's job specifications.
- Make known where all responsibilities lie.
- Utilize a staff training program.
- Encourage CAD-user meetings.
- Allow careers to progress through the attainment of CAD know-how.
- Give proficient CAD users encouragement.
- Develop user-friendly interfaces on the computers.
- Devise suitable working conditions.
- Inform CAD staff of the financial situation relating to them and their department.

5

Training

Some view training as something that is done at the early stages of one's life in preparation for "the real world." Others view training as an ongoing fact of working life, considering training's relationship to work as like that between gasoline and car. The latter grinds to a halt without the former.

Business seems to be accepting that the ongoing view of training is the most sensible approach — at least, in theory. In practice, however, training is often ignored. Chapter 13 examines why this is and presents the case for training by treating it like any other investment.

It is not just a matter of to train or not to train. What is needed is "effective" training. Chapters 14 and 15 look at how the desired objectives can be achieved with a little initial consideration followed by an appropriate training program.

Training is time-consuming and costly but also undeniably worthwhile. This part of the book shows how a company and its workforce can reap the maximum benefit from training.

13

The Case for Training

It is very difficult nowadays to find a business manager who does not propound the notion that training is not only desirable but vital if long-term business aims are to be realized and returns on staff investment optimized.

This opinion is not just held by those in management positions. The same enthusiasm for training is found in the persons who sit at the CAD terminals day after day. They realize that increased skills will allow them to perform their current duties with a greater proficiency and to "shift up a gear" into more stimulating work.

When, however, it comes to putting these common sentiments into practice, there is a noticeable lack of action.

Where CAD is involved, this is often because of computer-ignorant people asserting that "the computer does the work, not the operator," and that the user can "get on with the work and find out how to use it later on." These damaging misconceptions are clearly preposterous and must be tackled whenever apparent. A computer is nothing more than a box of electronics; the talent lies with the operator and must be nurtured at every opportunity.

A more pragmatic stumbling block hindering the good intentions is the financial justification of training. Unless this is overcome, the instinct for training will never be allowed to make headway.

In today's business environment, we are all very familiar with any expenditure first having to be justified objectively. Investment without short-term financial returns may well be considered a waste of resources.

This rationale is applied to all expenditure, including training, and so it is the people holding the purse strings who decide whether resources will be committed. Even if there is no outlay, such as in the case of in-house training by the CAD Manager, wages and overheads are still to be paid during periods of no production.

At best, training is viewed as a necessary overhead, and at worst, a cost that is first to be axed in any cost-cutting exercise.

The Financial Justification of Training

So how does the CAD Manager get training onto the business agenda? Unless the case for training can be argued for in harsh monetary terms, there will be great difficulty getting a training program off the ground.

Training must be justified as a worthwhile investment—as an expenditure that will benefit the business and create tangible financial rewards. This doesn't mean that training should automatically leap to the top of any business's list of priorities, but that it should be treated as an investment opportunity rather than a cost. The only true cost is the cost of *not* training.

Training as an investment

Too often companies approach training from the wrong direction: either as the result of staff pressure or the boss's gut instinct. In such circumstances, firms rarely bother to monitor or even expect any noticeable results from a training program. Consequently, the outcome will nearly always be expenditure without any corresponding returns, financial or otherwise.

Training and financial rewards are linked by the business objectives that training brings about. More and more business objectives can be met as the amount of appropriate training increases. This is shown in Fig. 13-1.

The financial benefits brought about by meeting these business objectives comes in two forms, as demonstrated in Fig. 13-2—either of which are sufficient to justify embarking on a training program. Firstly, costs can be cut by reducing the number of man-hours used to complete projects. Secondly, revenue can be increased by improving production. The correlation needs to be identified between training and any of the costs cut or revenue generated as a result of that training.

To see how this is applied in practice, consider the following all-too-common scenario:

A busy design company has staff working all hours. Designers sit at CAD equipment, feverishly generating plans and elevations one after another, while freelance visualizers create "realistic" views of the same project, all of which are presented to the client for approval.

The company manager realizes that the cost of CAD equipment and operators is high and the cost of employing freelance visualizers astronomic. Even so, the manager feels that they are getting value for money from both and that the company is keeping its head above water.

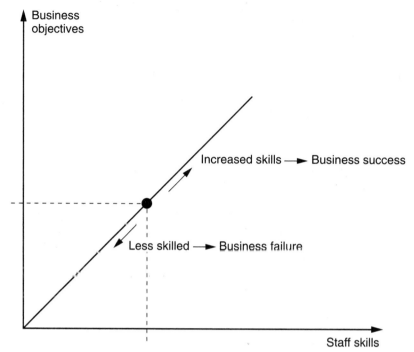

Figure 13-1. Appropriate training brings about business objectives.

However, the CAD staff feel disgruntled. They consider the CAD equipment and themselves vastly underutilized, and they resent money and praise being heaped on a visualizer when they know that they could do the job better and cheaper. All they require is training in 3-dimensional CAD techniques, and they will be able to create 3-D "models" rather than 2-D plans. Then they would be able to present the client with images of that 3-D model taken from any number of viewpoints.

The subject of training is frequently raised during conversations between the staff and the company manager, but he cannot see beyond their possibly selfish motives for training. He feels they will leave for higher paid jobs as soon as they have squeezed as much free training out of him as they can. The reality is, however, that they feel they are stagnating there and *will* leave *unless* they are allowed to develop with the help of training.

The CAD Manager plays an intermediary role between staff and senior management and argues the case for money to be spent on CAD training. So how can the case for training be presented? As discussed earlier, the only worthwhile arguments are those that relate to business objectives. Any accusations that training is required for purely

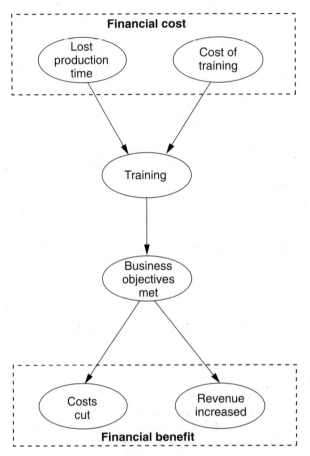

Figure 13-2. The financial justification of training.

personal advantage must be dispelled. Similarly, the CAD Manager must not appear to be "empire-building."

The way to link training investment to financial returns was shown in Fig. 13-1 by this simple correlation:

Training → Business objectives met → Financial benefit

Applying that to the scenario described here, the relationship would look like that shown in Fig. 13-3.

Though it may be difficult to attach actual figures to some of the business repercussions, the more quantifiable it can be made, the better. Appropriate training can be seen to increase productivity as well as broaden the scope of business activity. The company manager will be able to include the provision of 3-D CAD training for the staff along with other business decisions, whereas previously it was treated as a peripheral consideration never being allowed the opportunity to make serious headway.

This example involves a new skill replacing expensive and superfluous staff. Other circumstances may involve training being implemented simply to strengthen existing CAD skills. The route to increased profits would be by reduced mistakes and the increased flexibility of the CAD staff.

The cost of not training

Once the link has been made between appropriate training and realized business objectives, it becomes apparent that insufficient training is the cause of many business weaknesses. There is a cost of not training—the cost of failing to develop resources.

For instance, the CAD Manager's job description will usually include the brief to develop software and hardware capabilities. This activity is clearly desirable, as it can lead to both reduced costs and increased revenue. A new bit of software or a stunning piece of customization could save time, effort, and bring in new business, but this will not happen unless there are trained staff capable of putting the innovation to use.

The consequences of a lack of training are felt at all levels in the company. Concern is expressed from senior management that feel the CAD department is failing to perform, and the staff feel frustrated and pressured to do work for which they are inadequately trained.

Ask CAD users if they think that their company's CAD system is being fully used, and more than likely they will say no. Ask them if they think *they* are being fully used, and they are likely to say no. This sad fact would not be tolerated in any other business environment. Any machine that only performed to 50% of its capability even when demand for the product was high would be the subject of scrutiny until the problem was solved.

Companies may be getting a reasonable return on their CAD investment but only a fraction of the return that they could achieve if its

---

3-D Training —>

      increased staff motivation and retention
      reduced time and cost of the visualizer
      greater accuracy than with the visualizer
      increased productivity
      improved service offered (3-D design possibilities)
      increased competitiveness
      increased business

      —> Increased Profits

Figure 13-3. The repercussions of 3-D training.

potential were realized. The CAD Manager, CAD user, and company Manager often will be unaware whether or not they are fully exploiting their CAD system. It is through training that this question is answered and through training that potential can be realized.

What to Do

- Support managers who say that training will allow business objectives to be met.
- Support staff who say that training will increase their proficiency as well as make their work more stimulating.
- Justify training with tangible, objective figures.
- Treat training as an investment opportunity.
- Link training to financial rewards via the business objectives it brings about.
- Link insufficient training with business weakness and the cost of not training.

14

Prerequisites for Effective Training

Once the case for training, as discussed in the previous chapter, has been proven beyond reasonable doubt, one must consider how to make the most of the training opportunity.

Simply booking a half-day course at the local college is unlikely to give satisfactory results, because thought must be given to targeting the right type of training to the right people. The following chapter looks at the appropriateness of various training programs, but this one explains what should be considered prior to implementing any training, in order to maximize its effectiveness.

Issues such as the receptivity of individuals in the company to various methods of teaching, the content of any training course, when to put it into practice, and how to gauge its effect all help to ensure a focused and worthwhile training program.

The effect of these prerequisites on training and the subsequent effect on production is demonstrated in Fig. 14-1.

CAD-mindedness

It is alarmingly common for senior management to expect a manual designer to require only a short lesson at a CAD terminal to be transformed into a CAD designer. This is sometimes the way it happens, but only very rarely. The final objective of both drawing methods may be the same, but CAD requires a different thought process to drawing board techniques.

When training a group of manual designers, one of the first things an instructor realizes is that (put bluntly) not everyone can do it. There is such a thing as "CAD-mindedness" that some people do not possess— similar to the way some people can perceive a tune by looking at a

PRODUCTION

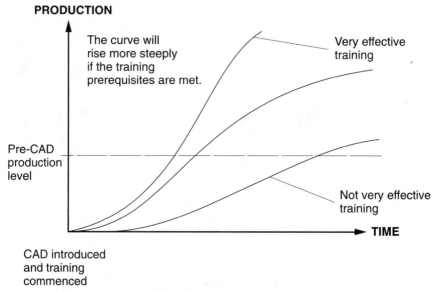

Figure 14-1. Increase in productivity due to training.

musical score, while others see it as a meaningless mess of tadpoles. To some, drawing can only involve pencil and paper, and a drawing in the form of computer data is a concept that they just cannot come to terms with.

While a few are absolutely incapable of doing the work, others feel threatened by CAD and more view it as a great puzzle. There is undoubtedly a fear of the unknown when people first sit at the CAD terminal.

Matters are made worse by the incorrect presumption that the student already possesses a certain amount of know-how. Missing out on a simple step of the course because of this may cause the whole course to fail. For example, if the student does not understand the concept of representing a point in space in terms of x, y, z coordinates, then she will never be able to come to grips with 3-dimensional CAD space.

Many accomplished designers have severely restricted themselves by using the computer as if it were a rectangular piece of paper the same size as the screen and using the "Line" command as their sole design tool, as if it were a pencil. It is no surprise that these people were not greatly impressed by the CAD facility!

Those previously untouched by computers often prefer to remain ignorant rather than feel as if they are going back to school. They may not even be aware of it, but a psychological block gets in the way of any enthusiasm they might have felt. Attempting to train these people in CAD techniques is a waste of time, unless it is a basic awareness course to allow them to work alongside CAD designers. In short, do not force people onto CAD who do not show any interest whatsoever in it.

Usually it is only the designer who is fully committed to CAD who can take full advantage of the training. Ironically, it is these people who are likely to read up, experiment, and push their personal and professional talents further *without* an organized training course.

Companywide Scope

Design technology has allowed more time to be spent on creative design work rather than the drawing and computation chores. This has led to the pure drafter's role diminishing as the scope of the designer has broadened.

These shifting roles must be considered when the training strategy is being planned. After deciding whether it is desirable to change a person's function in the company, one must consider whether additional training will be required to support the change in job specification. For example, this may take the form of instruction in company procedures that they will need to be familiar with, such as dealing with suppliers, Quality Assurance, or whatever.

Similarly, CAD is no longer restricted to the drawing office. The Accounts department, for example, may utilize CAD's computational abilities, or personnel may hold the office layout and staff details on a single, well-attributed CAD drawing. Training will therefore have to extend beyond the drawing office boundaries to encompass all areas of the company experiencing the consequences of CAD technology.

Following on from the fact that training should not be limited to those sitting at the CAD machines, there may be many in an organization who can benefit from training who do not directly experience CAD at all. For instance, it may be worthwhile for those at senior management level to be better informed on CAD — not about technical details, but rather about the implications of CAD on the company.

Appropriate Training Styles

The benefit gained from training varies according to the individual's ability to perceive the information been offered to them. Successful training methods must, therefore, correspond to those who are being trained.

There are three common styles of training, and the student will respond differently in each case.

Some may be most suited to a quick run through the basic commands, followed by hands-on experience working on practical work problems on their own. The trainer, acting more like a consultant, is on hand for any specific queries.

Others may find a formal teacher/student relationship more reward-ing. Here the instructor delivers a clear and structured curriculum, possibly followed by a test of some sort.

A third approach is to concentrate initially on getting to grips with the general concept of CAD so that students are familiar with this new "world" before they enter into it to carry out their work.

There is not one of these three styles that can be singled out as the best. It is really a matter of horses for courses—the best results being obtained by using the style most suited to a particular student.

Relevant Syllabuses

To reiterate the key statement from the previous chapter, "training must relate to business requirements." The same principle applies when deciding who to train. It is not good enough, no matter how well intentioned, to work around the office, training people just because it is their turn. Staff must be selected to receive training in order to achieve specified results.

Similarly, it is not simply a matter of the more staff that can be trained the better. Having more trained CAD users than can utilize the system is a waste. On the other hand, an insufficient number of trained staff results in an underutilized CAD system.

CAD tuition must take into account the organization in which the staff works and the type of work that they are involved in. Just being told what function each command performs does not constitute a train-ing program.

Ask yourself, "Why does X require training?" There is no point in explaining in detail every feature of a new piece of software if they only require it to perform a single task. If the student is an office space planner, for example, they are not interested in computing or the soft-ware per se, but are interested in office space planning alone and will only use CAD to perform this task better.

Similarly, there is no point in explaining how the computer network operates or demonstrating the hidden wonders of the operating system when the user is only concerned with where the ON switch is so that they can get on with their work. In short, make training specific and relevant to the person receiving the instruction.

As well as this, other factors such as computer literacy, CAD experi-ence, and personal confidence determine the most appropriate form of training for students to take. It is pointless spending time, money, and effort training a student who is not sufficiently competent to benefit from the knowledge being imparted. A special program for absolute beginners is worthwhile to get them going without hindering those already making progress. Sufficient practical experience of CAD must be gained at one level before moving on to more challenging areas.

Good Timing

A tactical time to invest in training is during a recession. Or—if you are blessed with the gift of predicting the future—just before the end of a recession. This has several advantages.

If you wish to use a training establishment, their prices will be very competitive, as they too will be feeling the effect of a downturn in business. This is a good opportunity to negotiate deals, possibly to adapt class size, timing, content, and price to your requirements.

Quiet times in the office allow more effective targeting of the training—that is, it is easier to schedule who and when to train.

During busy periods, time allotted to training members of staff is time during which work is not being done. In recessionary times, however, staff are being utilized more efficiently by being trained, as opposed to spending time less productively "shuffling papers."

A lull in activity gives the opportunity of assessing past effectiveness, the present situation, and where the company's future lies. Such a time is ideal for training staff with the skills necessary to take the company in the direction being charted.

Assessment

A successful training program will accomplish the goals it set out to achieve. Information acquired on how effective past training programs have been are useful when deciding future plans. As well as this, details of training courses including results should be made available to company management to assist their understanding of the training process.

There are three approaches that can be taken when assessing whether the required objectives have been met and the appropriate skills learned.

First, an assessment test similar to those described earlier in Chapter 11 could be given to students after completion of a course. A simple "before and after" comparison will yield the required information.

Second, assessment could take place through casual observations by the CAD Manager of staff carrying out their day-to-day tasks.

Third, the CAD Manager may prefer to wait until the time for existing staff review sessions to make an assessment. The acquiring of skills could even be incorporated into a "performance-related pay" calculation.

Skills can be rated individually and compared with preferred levels, maybe in chart form. This will indicate deficiencies, where training will need to be targeted, and underutilized skills that are being wasted.

What to Do

- Identify those who are sufficiently CAD-minded to benefit from training.

- Allow the training strategy to extend beyond the boundaries of the CAD drawing office.
- Match the style of the training to the student receiving it.
- Make syllabus content relevant to business objectives.
- Determine the best time to train.
- Assess the effectiveness of any training undergone.

15

Training Programs

The subject of computer-aided design is very wide as well as deep. That is, the broad scope of CAD applications that are available provides many starting points for those wishing to gain an insight, and, once interested, one can pursue the matter in great depth to learn more. Add this to the variety of people wishing to learn and their differing circumstances and you realize that selecting an appropriate training program is like selecting a pair of shoes — a very individual experience.

Types of Training Programs

Covered here are the numerous options available for accomplishing a training program, grouped to distinguish between "impersonal" ways (where a student follows a do-it-yourself method) and the "personal" ways (which allow dialogue and interaction between tutor and student).

Impersonal

There are many reasons why people prefer instruction to be impersonal. For instance, circumstances may dictate that it is not possible to allot long periods of time to study. The primary advantage of these methods is the chance to learn when and where you like, including at home.

Research shows that many people forget three-quarters of what they were taught just three days after a training class. Retention of information is likely to be greater with impersonal methods as they allow the opportunity to review the course at will.

Chapter 13 covered training in terms of investment, where the overall cost is compared with the financial reward. With the methods mentioned here, the initial outlay is relatively small, but there is the cost of the trainee being nonproductive during the training period, which must be included in any cost/returns calculations.

Videotapes A videotape, possibly a series of them, may convey the information using an instructor plus CAD screen images and other visual aids. They are usually preferred by those with limited budgets and inflexible schedules. Not only can videos be used individually, they can be viewed by a group of students in a single session. The videotapes may only comprise part of a larger training package that combines videotape, audio cassette, written text, and computer diskettes.

Software Commercially available software loaded onto the student's computer provides user-friendly programs of instruction and exercises to work through. The interface is by screen menus and icons as well as the standard CAD drawing editor. Topics are explained using a combination of on-screen text and graphics. The sophistication of these programs varies from the crude and simplistic to state-of-the-art interactive, multimedia experiences. Workbooks may be available to supplement the software. Once a software-based tutor has been purchased, it can be reused many times by different people or by past students wanting a refresher course.

A more recent development is a form of personal training via a modem. Examples are given, questions are asked, and work is set by the tutor at the end of the modem line.

Books Books are portable and once purchased can be referred to again and again. But do not think that it is only necessary to buy the book to acquire the knowledge. Books are not magic; they take time and effort to study.

There are a vast array of CAD tutorials on the market, so do not just grab the first one you see. Before you buy, look carefully through them to see what they cover and how the information is expressed. How up-to-date is it? What level of knowledge does it assume? Are more advanced books available to progress on to?

Manuals The official manual accompanying any CAD package should always be at hand, no matter how proficient the user. Although I wouldn't recommend that a beginner try to learn simply from this alone, it is very useful in association with other training methods.

In fact, I first gained my CAD knowledge with very basic classes, combined with solitary experimental sessions with the manual at my side. For example, the tutor would demonstrate the ability to Zoom in and out. Then, using the manual as a guide, I could explore all the other options within the Zoom command (window, extents, scale, and so on).

Personal training

This is the generally accepted method of training. The student being more involved with the process is able to ask questions, have bad habits corrected, and work to a discipline that many would be unable to manage without.

Distance learning Instruction and projects are delivered by mail. Although the work is performed away from class, there is regular communication between student and teacher. The course is structured and monitored by the training organization.

This method is best suited to those people who are self-motivated and have the commitment to continue the course to the end as sometimes the course duration can be lengthy. Impersonal distance learning courses are also available where one simply receives a pack containing the course module.

Seminars Sometimes held in association with exhibitions and product launches, or arranged by CAD suppliers, seminars provide a useful method of extending knowledge. They should not be used as the sole source of one's CAD education, however, and are most appropriate for CAD Managers wishing to investigate the latest software and hardware innovations.

In-house When a talented person in the company imparts their knowledge to another it results in the loss of productivity of two people over that period.

The "expert" doing the teaching may eventually find his work being dominated by tutoring duties. This would be unwise, as it reduces the time this talented person has for doing what he was originally employed to do. What's more, he isn't a qualified trainer, so it's quite possible that the training will be ineffective. He might know the CAD system inside out, but his ability to teach someone that has never encountered it before is by no means guaranteed.

The decision to rely on in-house training for a particular software package should rest on whether the software being used is bought-in or developed in-house. When the in-house staff that actually designed the package are offering the instruction, there is the added bonus of having them on hand in the future to answer any queries. It is beneficial for them also because it provides direct feedback from the people who use the software, helping them to improve their product.

Training establishments Formalized training establishments are more popular when there is a flexible and mobile workforce. This is because a company is then less inclined to commit themselves to long-term staff investment, such as training, and therefore relies on outside bodies for training provision.

This is particularly noticeable where workplace culture differs between countries. The USA and UK have a relatively mobile workforce, whereas in Japan, for example, workers stay at a single company for most of their working lives. Consequently Japanese companies tend to organize their own training.

Many training establishments exist but look out for those officially authorized by the manufacturer of your particular CAD software. Courses are usually structured to give a clear progression from one to another. Many special offers are available to entice companies to commit large numbers of trainees and to return for follow-up courses. A breakdown of the courses commonly available follows next.

Courses Held by Training Establishments

Training can be received from a variety of training establishments offering a wide range of training programs. Some may be specifically geared toward providing tailor-made training solutions for big business clients, while others may provide basic instruction and shared access to computers at evening classes held at a local school.

Examined here are courses generally available, along with topics they would include. The most common courses are those offering instruction in the computer-operating aspect of CAD. In practice these would be tied to a particular software, and the suppliers of that software should be able to help you find the right course for your needs.

Basic training for new users

For complete beginners, hands-on experience under the supervision of a skilled trainer is very worthwhile. The content of a basic course should begin with what to do from the moment one sits down in front of the computer, then cover basic drawing, editing, and viewing commands and finish off with how to output work done.

Sample syllabus is as follows:

- Equipment familiarization
- Entering new and existing drawings
- Menu and Tablet
- Precision input
- Drawing aids
- Entity creation and manipulation
- Linetypes
- Text
- Grouping entities
- Display commands
- Saving work
- Plotting

Intermediate training for existing users

Continuing from the previous course, or for self-taught users, this will investigate further the commands covered in the basic syllabus and go beyond into areas such as dimensioning and system variables.

Sample syllabus is as follows:

- Further 2-D editing techniques
- Dimension creation and manipulation
- Hatching
- Creating and extracting attributes
- Alternative ways to output work (plotfiles, DXF files, etc.)
- Coordinate systems for 2-D and 3-D space
- The 3-D environment
- Basic drawing in 3-D

Advanced training for existing users

A further development from previous courses. This syllabus will look into customization, particularly when it is intended for CAD Managers wishing to improve their system-customization skills. At this more advanced level, the instructor should possess a reasonable knowledge of the field of work the student is involved in.

Sample syllabus is as follows:

- 3-D drawing and editing
- Viewing 3-D images
- Surface modeling
- Solid modeling
- Customizing the drawing environment
- Customizing commands

Training in specific software

These courses are for capable CAD users wishing to include familiarity of specialist add-on software in their repertoire. It involves following a progression during the course(s) — beginner, intermediate, advanced — as with the basic CAD software.

The add-on software package could be, for instance, an architectural package that provides the user with an improved selection of tools with which to tackle building design projects, or maybe a rendering package that will allow the user to turn 3-dimensional wireframe drawings into presentable photo-realistic images.

Management training

The executives in a company that will not be using CAD themselves but making decisions that invariably involve CAD should attend this course. It will provide them with an awareness of the capabilities and implications of CAD throughout the workplace. The content of such a course would not be dissimilar to the contents of this book.

As with all of the courses mentioned in this chapter, the effectiveness is increased when the course relates to the specific business sector that the student comes from.

System management

In many companies, the role of CAD Manager will encompass the role of a System Manager and Network Manager as well. All computer networks possess idiosyncrasies, so it is necessary to be trained in the operation of one's own particular setup. This is just as true for small CAD setups as it is for large ones.

This training should normally be provided by the same organization that installed the system's hardware and software. As well as operation, it should include instruction on such everyday working procedures as backing up, archiving, and memory management.

Upgrade training

This course is available to teach those experienced in the current release of software about the new features of the latest upgraded version.

The decision of whether you actually want to upgrade in the first place is discussed in Chapter 17. If you do upgrade, then this training is essential and its cost should be taken into account when deciding to upgrade.

As well as new commands to learn, there are familiar commands that have been altered, plus whole new capabilities that will have been developed — all presented on new command menus. This must be understood even if the work to be done is the same as it was before the upgrade.

What to Do

Decide the most appropriate source of training:

- Videotape
- Software
- Books
- Manuals

- Distance learning
- Seminars
- In-house
- Training establishments

Exploit the variety of courses available at training establishments:

- Basic training for new users
- Intermediate training for existing users
- Advanced training for existing users
- Training in specific software
- Management training
- System management
- Upgrade training

6

The Workload

The combination of office procedures that aid the passage of work through the workplace, from the initial collation of relevant data to the eventual output of finished product, constitute the company's workload management policy.

It can be considered a "shop floor" area of management, directly involved with the product, as opposed to (say) financial management, which though important is a step removed from production.

Numerous overlapping tasks are involved in managing a company's workload, and they have been collated here under six distinct headings. There is nothing written in stone about the number or the title of these groupings; it is simply a convenient way to present and examine the full range of issues involved in this broad topic.

The full implications of each of the six subjects are discussed in their own right in their own chapter, as well as their importance to overall workload management:

- *Input: The appraisal of raw materials.*
- *Resources: The evaluation of personnel, software, and hardware.*
- *Data: The protection of CAD data integrity.*
- *Scheduling: The identification and organization of CAD work.*
- *Drawing: The drawing's standards and presentation.*
- *Output: The conclusion of the CAD design process.*

For reasons of clarity and continuity, the same six headings are referred to in Part 7: Project Planning. There, an individual project follows a route plan through the workload management issues discussed in this part of the book.

Chapter

16

Input

An advantage of CAD methods over manual techniques is the ease in which information from a variety of sources can be incorporated into the design work. As well as all of the sources known to manual drafters, there are increasing numbers of new ones that are becoming more familiar as design technology develops beyond the drawing office.

Input data constitutes the raw materials that will eventually be processed into something new. An inaccuracy or misunderstanding at this early stage can send the whole project off course. It is essential, therefore, that this data be properly assessed prior to use.

As there are numerous potential raw materials, so there must be a wide range of procedures to deal appropriately with them. Appraisal of the information may be performed by the Project Manager, the CAD Manager, the CAD designer, or someone else in the organization (job titles and descriptions vary from company to company).

In the long history of the drawing office, careful attention has always been paid to input material. There is a very real danger that, during the progression from drawing boards to computers, this practice will be forgotten. The assessment of initial information is as essential a concern now as it always has been, if not more so.

Here we will examine the form that the incoming data can take and then determine how it can be properly appraised.

Sources of Input

An obvious form of input for a CAD system is existing CAD drawings. These can be imported, either fully or in part, and incorporated in new work.

The data may derive from a past project with similar content. For instance, imagine a new job involving designing a gas station forecourt. The design would benefit from any experience gained from similar forecourt projects that the company had worked on previously. There will be elements, such as pump configurations, car-turning circles, and so on, that will provide excellent foundations for the new design work.

The client may supply information themselves in the form of a database taken from their own CAD system. If both systems are identical (or at least compatible), transference is very simple and straightforward. Simply copying files using floppy disks is easy enough, but if there is a great deal of data a modem link may be preferable, as it allows access to the bank of data whenever required. The subject of data transfer is discussed in depth in Chapter 8.

Where CAD systems differ, a straightforward translation process will usually be sufficient to make the data from one system accessible to the other. The commonly used translation facility is the DXF (Drawing Exchange Format) file, though new alternatives such as STEP (the STandard for Exchange of Product data) are entering onto the market all the time.

Nowadays it is quite possible that site information received from a surveyor will be in digital form and can be translated into CAD images using appropriate software. If surveyors still present their facts as paper drawings, they could be scanned into the CAD system. That is, an automatic translator will convert lines on paper into a digital format recognizable by a computer. Likewise, paper drawings from any other source, even hand sketches, can be scanned onto the CAD facility.

An alternative is for the CAD user to slavishly recreate the paper drawing on the computer. The operator can use a ruler to scale off measurements from the drawing and enter the data onto the CAD system. It is disheartening for a CAD designer to sit at a terminal and simply copy work that has been done already by a manual designer, but once the data is on the system, it may prove very useful to the designer.

Input Appraisal

When the various forms of input just described arrive at the design office, there are important things to consider that are more or less generally applicable. The process is simple: all potential input data must pass through an appraisal stage before being entered and used on the CAD system (see Fig. 16-1).

The following points should be borne in mind whenever new data is to be placed on the CAD system.

Alterations

Are there any unusual aspects of the input data that may involve applying techniques that require specialist skills or equipment? For example, a client's brief may request that their logo is included in all

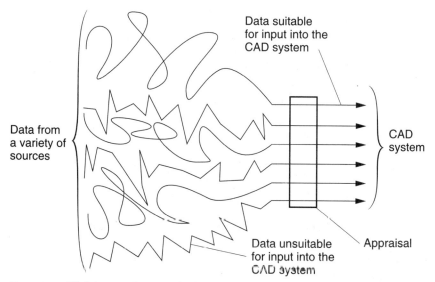

Figure 16-1. All data must be appraised prior to input into the CAD system.

the CAD drawings. Inputting this data may prove awkward if their logo is complex.

Justification

When data is put onto the CAD system, and alternative courses of action could have been taken, it means a decision has been made to input that particular data. When this is so, that decision should be justified. For instance, if a particular style of furniture is incorporated into a design — possibly from a symbol library — the reason for choosing it should be made clear. Otherwise, the choice may be made for purely expedient reasons.

Quality and accuracy

For some reason, data is commonly assumed to be of the highest quality and accuracy simply because it is presented from an outside source. However, it is because of this that one must be wary of it. The quality and accuracy of all newly acquired data should be monitored.

Conventions and standards

Many companies using CAD techniques have their own in-house conventions and standards defined for such things as dimensioning and layering. It is important that any imported CAD data also conforms to these same rules. This will often create additional work for either the supplier of the data or for the company receiving it.

Preparatory work

Any modification or translation of input data subsequent to receiving it requires effort to be expended before even beginning the design stage of the work. The amount of effort required will place a corresponding strain on the company's resources. It is important, therefore, to avoid the trap of a project with a disproportionate amount of preparatory work.

File details

When CAD information is received from its source on floppy disk, details such as filenames, file contents, and subdirectories should be apparent. A disk in the hands of someone less familiar with computers may otherwise not convey all of the information it is intended to. Also, disks can easily be misplaced and damaged. A printout of the information each disk contains and the project it relates to will greatly help to avoid losing of valuable data.

Traceability

Similarly, any documentation accompanying data received should be monitored and cared for in a controlled way. It's easy to lose track of data and its sources deep into a long project. Input material should be accessible to all and be as traceable as is feasibly possible.

Discrepancies

Particularly when architectural work is involved, various survey information must often be contended with. If surveys are arriving from more than one source, discrepancies may occur in symbols used and levels of accuracy. If this information is being fed directly into the CAD system, there is a danger that different survey conventions will be incorporated into one drawing.

If possible, demand a universal standard from all sources. If this is not possible, then one must be alert to inconsistencies and willing to modify irregular input data.

Verification

Transference of data between two dissimilar CAD systems using an intermediate filetype, such as a DXF file, may result in information being altered "en route" or (at worst) lost altogether. Verifying the completeness of any such transfer is best achieved by referring to a hard copy of the drawing being transferred. When receiving a drawing exchange file from an outside source, always request an accompanying printout for verification purposes.

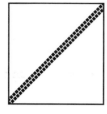

A magnified view of a line drawn on paper

A reproduction of the above after it has been poorly scanned into the CAD system

An accurate reproduction of the line as it should appear on the CAD system

Figure 16-2. Scanning lines on paper into CAD data.

Similarly, data received through a modem connection must also be checked for completeness and accuracy. The transmission parameters of both transmitter and receiver modems must be known. Output quality varies between systems, so there is plenty of scope for incompatibilities. A common problem occurs when information is transmitted at a rate beyond that which it can be received.

False economies

Apparent time-saving procedures may create more work than expected. For example, converting paper drawings into computer data using scanning technology is increasing in popularity as the technology has advanced and become more accessible. There are a wide variety of scanning procedures and a corresponding variety of quality (see Fig. 16-2).

Thoroughly investigate the capabilities of a scanning process before committing to it. It is not uncommon for work scanned into a CAD system to save time to produce an image consisting of feathery, multiple lines (and hence an astronomical filesize) instead of the single sharp lines expected. This results in a tired CAD designer having to redraw the entire scanned image. This is certainly not true for all scanning systems, but be warned that scanning is not always as straightforward as one might think.

What to Do

- Ensure that the skills and equipment needed to modify incoming data are available if necessary.
- Verify that data is used because it enhances the design process and not just because it is from an easily available source.
- Monitor the quality and accuracy of all incoming data.
- Maintain in-house conventions and standards.
- Avoid unnecessary preparatory work.
- Catalog filenames, etc., to avoid "misplacing" data.
- Look for discrepancies in the drawing conventions of data from different sources.
- Check the completeness of incoming data, possibly using a paper printout for verification.
- Make sure that apparent time-saving procedures (such as scanning) do not in practice increase the workload.

17

Resources

Resources are the stock on which a business draws to fulfill its work commitments. Even when resources are insufficient, projects are often still pursued, as if the necessary resources will fall into place once the project progresses. The relationship between the resources available and the project's requirements is demonstrated in Fig. 17-1. To avoid the shortcomings and conflict that will inevitably occur when resources do not match requirements it is essential to carry out an accurate assessment of resources before a project commences.

The resources relevant to the field of computer-aided design come under three headings: personnel, software, and hardware. Details of both software and hardware must be documented and held by the CAD Manager, possibly as part of the company's Quality Assurance policy. Up-to-date personnel details, such as training and work experience, should also be on record. This information will be held by the Personnel Manager though the CAD Manager should also possess details of all staff using the CAD facility.

This intelligence gathering is necessary to allow the successful evaluation of resources. Evaluation is necessary to indicate any deficiency that would hinder the successful completion of a project.

Once any shortfall has been identified, the financial and practical considerations of strengthening the existing resources can be considered. These must be resolved before any firm commitment is made to a project.

Personnel

The skill level of the staff must at least match that necessary to complete the work ahead. If not, either the job requirements or the skill level must change. That is, the skills of the workforce must correspond to the skills demanded by the project to be tackled.

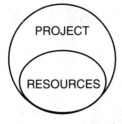

The project requires
greater resources than
those available. → Reduce
the scale of the project
or improve the resources.

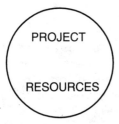

The resources match project
requirements. → The project
can be attempted but there
are no additional resources
for unforeseen circumstances.

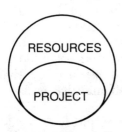

Resources exceed project
requirements. → The project
can be completed "better" or
resources can be used on other
projects.

Figure 17-1. The relationship between available resources and project requirements.

It is easy for a skills mismatch to occur, especially where CAD-ignorant people are involved in bringing the work into the company. For example, the marketing department may bring in a job where the client has specifically instructed that it be carried out using the same CAD package used by their company. The marketing department are pleased because they picked up on the buzzword "CAD," and they know that there are a lot of "computer whiz kids" in the design department, so it will be easy. Just sit a few of them down in front of the computers and the work will be done.

Their ignorance can cause major difficulties. A collection of the finest AutoCAD brains in the country sitting in the office is virtually worthless if the CAD system they are expected to work with is one that they have never encountered. This is akin to expecting a person fluent in French to translate a document written in Spanish.

Staff constitute a resource of a magnitude greater than that which is immediately obvious.

Consider all the training they have received and their work experience before and since joining the company. For example, if a project involved a lot of work abroad (say, in Greece), there may be a member of staff that has lived and worked there. This person would be an extremely valuable resource, as she could offer assistance in everything from the language barrier to Greek business practices and cultural idiosyncrasies.

Of course, one has to be careful not to be overly optimistic and make unreasonable demands on personnel. Remember that this resource is human. You may think it fair to offer a bit of extra vacation in return for a few all-night and all-weekend shifts, but physical limitations, headaches, eyestrain, and so on will make such things impossible, no matter how conscientious the staff. As with other resources, pushing staff too hard will only have a detrimental effect.

Software

Are existing software capabilities appropriate to the needs of the incoming project? Maybe new software is needed or perhaps upgrading existing software will be sufficient.

The cost of a new software package can be compared to the costs it will save and the revenue it will generate. It should also be noted whether the new software is likely to be of use in future projects as well as the current one.

Add-on software packages can complement the standard CAD software. There is a wide variety of "secondary" CAD software available to help automate otherwise time-consuming tasks. It ranges from the general facility, such as a symbol library, to the on-off time-saver, such as an automated batch of keyboard strokes. The latter would be of great value if, for example, a client requested all output to be in the form of DXF files. They may prefer this to straightforward CAD files or paper printouts because it allows easy transference into different CAD systems. This could mean a great deal of time-consuming DXFing for the designer to contend with. However, that can be avoided by using a simple add-on program that, when activated, will carry out the same task quickly and automatically.

Customization techniques can be employed to adapt existing software to relate more closely to the current tasks. For instance, if all the work is to be presented at scale 1:100, with specific line thicknesses and colors, in an A3 border with the client's logo in the top left-hand corner, a customized program can accomplish this "in the background" with a routine that runs automatically every time a drawing is printed.

During software discussions with a supplier or when researching software from magazines, a great deal of jargon can obscure the practicalities of the issue. The glossary in the back of this book should help you decipher some of these technical terms.

Software compatibility may prove troublesome even if the CAD software packages are the same. That is, problems may arise if there is a discrepancy in the version of the two software packages. This raises the question of upgrading.

Upgrading software: Is it worth it?

Most software producers release upgraded versions from time to time. In the case of AutoCAD, the best-selling CAD software, an enhanced version is released approximately every two years. This serves the vendor in two ways. Firstly, it keeps their product up-to-date and competitive; secondly, it provides a regular, ongoing income. If they just sold the software "once," they would soon run out of people to sell it to. Upgrades allow them to continue selling to the same buyer year after year who, possibly without realizing it, became committed to this recurrent expense when the initial purchase was made.

Implementing and modifying a CAD system with software and hardware that is suited to tackling the company's workload takes a lot of time and effort. There is, therefore, understandable resentment when the supplier explains that the software needs to be replaced by a more recent version, and those who do not purchase the upgrade will be left behind, stranded, and isolated.

The cost of the software upgrades is not only considerable but compounded by the additional costs of installation, additional training, and the slowed work rate during this time. There will be new commands, old ones that have been altered, new menus to negotiate, and completely new capabilities. All these things must be understood, even if the work to be done with the system is the same as before the upgrade. In short, the cost, degree of sophistication, and rate of change of today's CAD software makes upgrading a traumatic event. Is it worth it?

Of course, it may not be an issue. Upgrading may be necessary to perform a desired function. If you wish to take on 3-dimensional work, for instance, and only have a 2-dimensional capability, upgrading will be the sensible course of action.

When there is no obvious need to upgrade, the fear of storing up problems for the future by breaking the continuity now is usually a sufficient threat to cajole most people into complying with the supplier's wishes.

Replacing the megabytes worth of software that comprise a sophisticated CAD package, much of it tailored to the needs of that particular setup, is disruptive to say the least. As well as the installation and training already mentioned, system errors and software bugs also mark an upheaval of this magnitude.

Also, a software upgrade may incur a hardware upgrade. Extra hard disk space, RAM, processor speed, and so on may be necessary to cope with the new software. Failure to tackle this problem may result in a system with the latest and most powerful software but a CAD system that is slower and weaker than before.

The rational way to decide on upgrading is to ignore fashion and fads and base the decision on how well it will meet business objectives. All CAD-related purchases must be made on a businesslike basis. Buy only what meets business needs and what can be afforded. It would be crazy to let journalists' reviews, exhibition demonstrations, or an irrational desire for state-of-the-art technology to be the justification for such a significant course of action.

Be aware of contributions to business objectives from indirect sources. For example, an improvement in a software's "user-friendliness" may improve accessibility to CAD and reduce the need for training.

If you do decide to upgrade, an initial delay is advisable, with two advantages. First, waiting for a lull in workload allows for upgrading problems to be tackled and for users to experiment and learn the system. Second, it is common for the first release of an upgrade to contain faults or bugs; waiting for a subsequently revised release will ease the worry of glitches during work.

Finally, the question of upgrading provides a good argument for leasing CAD equipment. An upgrade can be incorporated into the leasing agreement. A mixture of owned and leased equipment will provide the best of both worlds.

Hardware

Is the free space on the hard disk sufficient? How suitable is the existing RAM?

These sort of questions need to be asked before the work gets under way, rather than waiting for trouble to hit midproject.

There are many aspects of computer hardware that need to be borne in mind when considering if it is up to the task ahead. As well as the basic standards for measuring computing power (RAM, mips, processor speed, etc.), there is the additional peripheral hardware to consider. For instance, a client may supply information, such as a data bank of symbols, on a CD-ROM disk. This is worthless unless there is a CD-ROM player available to access the information.

Output equipment, such as plotters (pen, electrostatic, laser), paper, film, disks, tapes, and modems must also be included in any assessment. The output is what the design process is all about, so the media used for drawing printouts is all-important. Whatever the specific form this media takes, the two major things to consider are availability and quality. Availability is something that must be guaranteed by the supplier. Quality refers to the media's response to the potentially damaging effects of such things as time, heat, and cold.

Weakness of the CAD setup is not welcomed by anyone, particularly the CAD designers. To them, a small shortfall in hardware capability can mean the difference between exploiting the design facility and unfulfilled potential. "Unfulfilled potential" refers to the opportunities kept out of the designer's grasp by avoidable hardware limitations, such as the following example.

Drawing in 3-dimensional CAD is similar to model making. It is a complex procedure creating a "model" but once created, there are infinite possibilities for viewing, plotting, and rendering. The "difficult bit" is doing the initial drawing work on the CAD system. Exploiting this effort is predominantly a matter of possessing suitable hardware. That is, a great piece of design work may have been created, but inadequate hardware can make it impossible to plot a single view. This is analogous to having expert model makers in a well-equipped workshop creating a magnificent structure, and then, after having built the structure, discovering that it won't fit through the door.

One method of evaluating the hardware resource and identifying possible shortcomings is to use a typical drawing from a project and to note access time, regeneration time, hidden line removal time, plot time, and so on.

There are commercially available benchmark tests that perform this task automatically and more thoroughly than manual methods could. There will be some preliminary questions to be answered about the system's hardware and configuration, including everything from CPU speed to the version of the CAD software. A typical mix of CAD commands are issued automatically. The resulting data is recorded in a series of report files — usually including a textural summary of results as well as a graphical representation of data.

The information provided from benchmark tests can be very useful. It provides something objective with which to measure and compare CAD hardware when making a purchase. Weaknesses can be identified in system performance due to specific elements such as the maths coprocessor, the VDU card, or the hard disk. When changes are made in the hardware or software setup, they can be evaluated using the same benchmark test.

Even more so than with software, hardware carries with it a plethora of acronyms, jargon, and techno-speak that seems designed to make the subject unfathomable. The glossary should help you make some sense of this gobbledygook.

What to Do

- Ensure that the skills of the workforce match the skills demanded by the project.

- Software capabilities must be appropriate to cope with the nature of the workload.

- Assess all aspects of CAD hardware for maximum effectiveness (hard disk, RAM, mips, processors, accelerators, all the peripherals, and the various output equipment and media).

18

Data

CAD has brought about a situation where drawings can easily and accidentally be duplicated or deleted. The possibility arises of designers unwittingly working on the same drawing held in more than one file and a lifetime's work being lost at the press of a button.

Then there is the hardware. No company is immune to computer breakdown. Anything from a bomb to a cup of coffee inadvertently spilt can cause a major setback.

Such pitfalls in the system need to be avoided in some way. Working methods must be known and formalized to ensure that the design information (that is, the files and the data contained in those files) remains safe and reliable.

Effective procedures, usually devised and implemented by the CAD Manager, constitute a valuable resource that allows a business to successfully manage its workload by guaranteeing data integrity. They play a part in a company's guarantee of quality to a client and are consequently mentioned in the "Quality Assurance" part of this book, covering the procedures in the QA policy documents.

Recovery of data is the key to surviving a computer breakdown and is where the existence of an efficient data back-up procedure proves its worth. Even if equipment must be hired at short notice, the foresight of keeping a safe copy of the data means that the work done is unharmed and available to allow the project to continue.

A common way of dealing with system faults is to make support agreements with external organizations. Even so, there should still be procedures for in-house support to implement preventative action, such as cleaning the plotter once a week.

Many aspects of the CAD facility's security, such as the prevention of burglary, fire, flood, power surges, and so on are dealt with by companywide policies. This chapter concentrates on the aspects of security relating specifically to a project's CAD data.

So, yes, data can be trusted, if the procedures described in this chapter are incorporated into everyday working methods.

Current Drawing File Management

Procedures have always existed in the drawing office for naming, cataloging, and monitoring work in progress. With the advent of CAD, this is even more vital, as there now exists not just drawings but differing versions of drawings and components of drawings. The result is a mass of similar but separate drawings. Organizing them is made more awkward by the fact that the drawings are not pieces of paper that can be held in the hand. They are invisible and intangible things that exist only in the memory of the computer.

Order rather than chaos

In an organization where many people are working on many projects and no structured method for storing drawing files on computer exists, files soon start to "disappear."

Not only that, monitoring of the work becomes impractical, resulting in a blissful ignorance about any shortcomings, errors, or incompetence.

Locating specific files on a CAD system must be easy — especially when numerous projects are being worked on simultaneously. The best way to accomplish this is to use a structured system of "directories" or "folders" as they are called on IBM-compatible and Macintosh computers respectively.

One person should be identified as having the authority to modify the file/directory/folder structure. However, the actual naming of drawings is not really for the CAD Manager or the CAD department to decide. It is a projectwide concern including all those that are involved in it and would normally be instigated by the Project Manager after consultation with project team leaders (including the CAD Manager). The naming system must be usable and workable by all those likely to encounter it.

Failure to consult can lead to trouble. For instance, it is no good if the Project Manager devises a naming scheme using 9-digit codes if the CAD system will only accept 8-digit codes.

Provision can be made to distinguish between differing versions of the work so that the correct file is accessed each time. This may be achieved by incorporating codes to indicate the drawing's stage of development — such as "preliminary sketch," "unfinished," "obsolete," "issued," and so on.

Naming drawings

Consider all aspects of the project when deriving a naming system. It is worth the effort devising a suitable system at the outset of a project rather than creating confusion and practical problems by changing systems midproject.

Whatever information is required should be contained in the drawing's name. There is no value in the inclusion of superfluous detail. What is required will vary with the nature of the project. Here is a typical example of a drawing name used in a design practice:

RTFINLIG03

So what does it mean? All names on this project consist of 10 alphanumeric characters. The first character denotes the department heading the project. In a design company, those departments may be:

R Retail

P Product

C Corporate

G Graphics

E Environmental

The next character denotes the client—in this case the supermarket chain "Thomson."

T Thomson

The following three characters refer to the site of the store. As the project involves many different sites, each must be identified:

FIN Finchley

BRE Brent

LUT Luton

BED Bedford

The next three characters signify the subject of the drawing:

LIG Lighting

ELE Electrical

FLO Flooring

UTI Utility

The final two digits indicate a specific area of concern. So, if Lighting needed four separate drawings to provide sufficient detail for the project, then these would be numbered LIG01 to LIG04:

LIG01 External

LIG02 Ceiling

LIG03 Checkout

LIG04 Display

Thus, RTFINLIG03 is the checkout lighting drawing for the Finchley store. The client is Thomson and the project is being coordinated by the Retail design department.

The drawing's name will appear in the title block. Revisions made to completed drawings will also be indicated in the title block.

Computer filing

Any common element can be removed from the drawing name when it is adapted into a computer filename. For instance, if the project name is indicated by the directory or folder name, it needn't be included in the filename as well.

In the previous example, RTFINLIG03, the name given to the CAD drawing file as used on the computer, can omit the first two (RT) or even first five (RTFIN) characters. The information conveyed by these five characters — "Retail, Thomson, Finchley" — is instead indicated by the directory/folder structure. So now the drawing file would be called LIG03 and be stored in the computer under RETAIL\ THOMSON\FINCHLEY, as indicated in Fig. 18-1.

Old Drawing File Management

CAD drawing files that are no longer in use are either:

Dead files: Unwanted, removed during regular hard disk "house-keeping."

Back-up files: The penultimate state of the file, the most recent being the file currently in use.

Archive files: Files from past projects, removed from the hard disk and stored elsewhere, often off-site, not intended to be accessed frequently.

Backing up

A well-constructed procedure for copying completed and ongoing work must be frequent, thorough, and workable. The data held on these back-ups should be identified by notes accompanying the back-up media (disks, tapes, etc.). The media must be tested regularly to confirm that all is well.

A successful back-up policy involves the combination of two different elements: full and incremental.

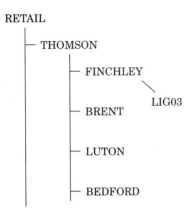

RETAIL
- THOMSON
  - FINCHLEY
    - LIG03
  - BRENT
- LUTON
- BEDFORD

Figure 18-1. Example file location in a directory structure.

Full back-ups copy everything from the hard disk to the removable media. A full drawing back-up would, therefore, involve making a copy of every drawing file that is held on the hard disk.

Incremental back-ups only concern files that have been modified since the last full back-up. An incremental drawing back-up would, therefore, augment existing back-up data with any drawings that have changed since it was made.

In practice, this could mean duplicating everything on the computer onto a tape at the end of each week. As well as this, at the end of every working day, work done during the week would be copied onto another tape.

The use of incremental back-ups are less time-consuming and more effective than relying on, say, full back-ups made daily onto separate tapes. When disaster strikes, at worst, only a day's work has been lost. If this is unsatisfactory, then incremental backups can be performed more frequently — twice a day, for example. Refuse to back up only work that you are prepared to lose.

Operating systems vary, as do users' requirements. A company may use numerous levels of back-up to safeguard its work. The back-up schedule shown in Fig. 18-2 uses three levels:

Level 1: Full back-up (all system files and drawing files)

Level 2: Partial back-up (all drawing files)

Level 3: Incremental back-up (files modified since previous Level 1 and Level 2 back-ups)

The schedule covers four weeks with the back-ups taking place at the end of the indicated working day.

	MONDAY	TUESDAY	WEDNESDAY	THURSDAY	FRIDAY
WEEK 1	3	3	3	3	2
WEEK 2	3	3	3	3	2
WEEK 3	3	3	3	3	2
WEEK 4	3	3	3	3	1
WEEK 5	Repeat from week 1				

Figure 18-2. A schedule for backing up work.

All of the level 2 back-ups collect the data created since the level 1 back-up at the end of work on Friday at the end of the four-week cycle. All of the level 3 back-ups collect data created that week, since the previous Friday's back-up.

For greater security, each level's tapes (assuming that tapes are being used as the back-up media) should not be reused until the more complete level of back-up has been completed. For instance, in the previous example, Level 3 tapes can be reused after the weekly Level 2 back-up has been performed.

Restoring information is simply a matter of retrieving the desired files from the most up-to-date back-up. When restoring everything, restore the "incremental" AFTER the "full" to ensure the most recent files are not overwritten by older versions with the same name.

Backups are duplicates made for safeguarding recent work. Long-term storage of data requires the different procedure of archiving.

Archiving

As with backing up, the archiving procedure begins with copying the desired files onto tape, disk, or whatever, checking that the copies are accurate and error-free and then labeling the media and recording the filenames in an archive register. The big difference is that the original files are then deleted from the hard disk. The archive is the only version in existence.

Archiving a CAD project is usually the responsibility of the CAD Manager after consultation with the relevant Project Manager. It would normally be performed once the project has been completed and the need for further access to the work is not expected.

It must be remembered that, because the data is in long-term storage, restoration of the data must be possible long after the archiving procedure has taken place.

If, for example, a company archived their CAD work onto tape, then at a later date purchased new equipment for storage (such as optical disks), the data on tape must either be transferred to optical disk or an available tape drive. Otherwise, the archived material would be inaccessible.

With the rapid progress of design technology, such scenarios are very likely in the cases of both hardware and software.

To avoid this problem, ensure that any new hardware purchased has the ability to read archived data. It is also wise to make all archives in a "neutral" format — such as DXF or STEP files — that will be compatible with a variety of software packages.

Another matter for concern is the problem of the archive media simply decaying. It is hard to imagine someone restoring work done today in 100 years. Even so, that's the purpose of archiving, and the media must be stored in suitable circumstances.

Note the instructions on the specific back-up medium's packaging regarding maximum and minimum temperature, the effects of stray electromagnetic fields, and so on. Copying archives onto fresh media (say, once a year) is one way of increasing longevity.

An often forgotten concern is the life span of the labels. Using labels that eventually fall off the media or pens whose ink fades over time is no good — especially if common filenames are used on different projects. (If labels become detached, how can archived files be distinguished when each disk contains files with the same names — site1, site2, site3, for example?)

Fault Recovery

One disadvantage of CAD is that designers suffer from computer problems as well as the more familiar design difficulties. It is always hard to come to terms with lost or damaged data, but it still happens, whether through user negligence, virus infiltration, or unauthorized user intrusions. With some knowledge and forethought, faults can be minimized and the chances of recovery can be increased.

Restoring lost data

Anyone who has ever used a computer will recognize this scenario: It is 11 P.M. on Friday and the work that has kept you tied to the computer has finally been completed. Now all you need to do is delete the junk files created during the day's work. But a few seconds later, you see that you've deleted the very thing that you have been working on for so long. One moment of optimism says, "Well, I've done the work, so it must be here somewhere," but then your heart sinks as you realize the file has, in fact, been removed from the system.

Thankfully, there is no need to fret. Numerous software packages are available for retrieving "lost" data, and some organizations are devoted to recovering even the most tricky data. Even some files on a reformatted disk can be raised from the dead.

It is wise to have these software utilities handy for when they might be required. One popular choice is the Norton Utilities program set, which covers all common requirements — including unerasing files.

Of course, the best solution is to avoid getting to this stage in the first place. Instead of deleting files, it is a good idea instead to place them in a "waste bin" directory/folder which is only "emptied" once a month.

Virus protection

A source of nightmares among CAD Managers, and anyone else involved with computers for that matter, are computer viruses. There are hundreds of these and they are multiplying.

Prevention is definitely the best form of cure, and the best form of prevention is a virus-checking software program. Once the hard disk has been checked and cleared of any viruses, the program can be used to check any floppy disks before they come into contact with the system.

Use of the virus checker facility must be compulsory. It is not too troublesome and can be incorporated on a utility menu to make it simpler still.

If staff wish to bring computer games and other programs to work, keep such things off the CAD system until they have been cleared by the virus checker. An alternative is to provide a detached PC specifically for all nonoffice software.

Restricting access to data

The problem of unauthorized access is not just limited to "professional" hackers. Everyone is naturally curious — especially talented computer users wishing to put their abilities to the test.

A password system can restrict access to the CAD system to those with their names on the register of authorized users. Access may be allowed to the CAD system but not to all the data held on it. This might mean blocking access to any system files, customized programs, and confidential business such as staff reviews and so on. A representation of the access given to areas of the CAD database is shown in Fig. 18-3.

Trouble can start when staff are given partial access — or just partial knowledge — of confidential data. This can prove too tempting and encourage further prying. Also, beware of spiteful dispossessed staff who have reason to seek revenge; it's never too difficult to create mayhem on a computer system when one is in the mood.

One way to restrict access of a thief or anyone else to the information held by a computer is to "encrypt" the data using an automatic routine.

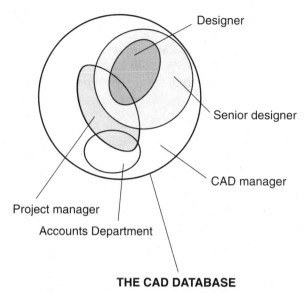

Designer

Senior designer

CAD manager

Project manager

Accounts Department

THE CAD DATABASE

Figure 18-3. Restricted access to the CAD system.

This makes any sensitive data unintelligible without the appropriate program to restore it.

A deleted file is not as inaccessible as you may think, but can be resurrected as mentioned previously. This trick is often used by data thieves. A seemingly innocent blank disk that they are carrying may contain deleted files that can be undeleted using another computer outside the office. So, when important files need to be permanently removed from a disk, erase them completely with an erasing program created specially for the task.

External support

No matter how sophisticated a CAD setup, the support of a specialist is invaluable for squeezing the most out of a system over its full life expectancy and for being there when disaster strikes and a helping hand is needed. The choice of who is to provide this support should be carefully considered.

Commonly a contract is signed with the company that supplied and installed the CAD software. An annual fee is paid, the size of the fee being proportional to the risk borne by the supplier. A range of contracts may be offered providing different degrees of support.

An alternative is to do it yourself. Though risky, it can be done. A good system knowledge is needed, as well as some diagnostic software. If the problem cannot be solved, an engineer can then be called in.

It is possible to shop around each time assistance is required. This docs allow more freedom of choice than a contract, but the continuity that a single organization providing the total support needs for the CAD department brings is a big advantage.

The main points to consider when choosing a support contract are as follows:

- *The quality of support offered:* Is it just telephone support from whomever is there at the time, or will they send an expert over to you in minutes?

- *The level of support offered:* Do they assist with CAD software problems as well as computer hardware failures?

- *The range of software supported:* Do they cover add-on packages as well as the core software?

- *The range of hardware supported:* Will they include plotters and network paraphernalia in the contract?

- *Their experience of the CAD industry:* Do you feel confident that they are completely familiar with CAD's specific requirements and problems?

- *Their suitability to your company's working methods:* You may work shifts — will they respond to a call for help in the middle of the night?

Go over the contract with a fine-toothed comb. Each contract is only as strong as its weakest link.

What to Do

- Name drawings using an informative and intelligible system.
- Adapt this appropriately to computer filenaming.
- Use a structured system of directories (or folders for Macintosh computers).
- Back-up data to removable media, such as tape or disk, according to a fail-safe back-up schedule.
- Archive past projects by removing them from the hard disk and storing them elsewhere, preferably off-site.
- Use preventative methods where possible to preempt the loss or damage of data by computer viruses, unauthorized access, etc.

- When problems do occur, have procedures in place to deal with them.

- Organize an external support contract to help safeguard against such pitfalls.

19

Scheduling

In the real world, as opposed to the one where we would like to live, companies are not fully committed to CAD. They are understandably cautious, testing the water before they commit themselves. Some are barely dipping their toes in, some are up to their waist, and a small number have dived in head first.

So when we talk of the workload, it is wrong to presume that it is based entirely around CAD. New design technology will most likely be sharing the workload with traditional methods.

Any incoming work, therefore, needs to be examined and allocated to either CAD working methods, traditional techniques, or a combination of both.

As well as this, the current commitment of resources needs to be considered. A schedule indicating the availability of all resources, including staff, over the forthcoming period can be created after regular consultation between the CAD Manager and project managers.

This chapter covers the suitability of projects and the existing workload schedule as far as CAD is concerned. A job can only be considered a priority for the CAD system after first examining these prerequisites.

CAD or Manual Methods?

When a prospective project is little more than a glint in the Marketing Manager's eye, it is necessary to consider whether it is to be tackled fully or partially on the CAD system, or not at all.

Where both methods are to be used in cooperation, a clear division of labor should be made and strictly adhered to. Poor job demarcation can lead to problems. It is typical in drawing offices that do not schedule their work appropriately for work completed on the CAD system to then be revised by hand, thus putting it in limbo — neither belonging to the CAD or manual design approach.

So, unless the company is fully committed to modern design technology, without a drawing board in sight, a choice of what work should be allocated to the CAD system and what work should not needs to be made.

This decision may be made for each new drawing, but, to fully utilize the CAD investment, it is best if it is made for the whole project — that is, "Is the whole project to be a CAD project or not?" This allows a coherence that would not be possible with the clashes and confusion arising when two different approaches are followed simultaneously.

What work is suited to CAD?

A common way of identifying work most suited to CAD is by looking for repetitive elements in the drawing (phases, floors, components). This is a very simplistic approach, and there is nothing wrong with that, but it should not be used to eliminate more complex drawings from the CAD workload. For instance, work may involve the interrelation of complex curves. CAD has the clear advantage here, as it is able to calculate and create them with 100% accuracy. Traditional methods, on the other hand, would require reams of mathematical calculations and guesswork to achieve a result that would be more "artistic" than accurate.

Less obvious are parts of the drawing that become repetitive elements after CAD transformations have been performed on them. Look out for symmetry, rotations, scaling, and so on.

When beginning completely new drawings, unless they contain the sort of repeated details just mentioned, CAD is often slower than manual methods. It is when it comes to modifying existing work that its speed advantage becomes apparent. Therefore, when analyzing incoming work, consider if there are likely to be many changes during the design process. In most cases the answer is yes, which means that the CAD approach is worthwhile.

Often the form that the input data takes will dictate whether or not the work will be done on CAD. As discussed in Chapter 16, input data may come from numerous sources. For instance, data from a client's CAD system or from a digital survey is particularly suited to computerized working methods.

New work may have similarities with previous projects tackled on the CAD system. Indeed, it may require simply modifying previous CAD work. In such cases, it would be foolish not to exploit this existing store of information by also placing the new work on the CAD system.

That involves looking to past projects, to determine what happens after the completion of the new project. Is the future use of the CAD data likely? For instance, if parts lists and "bill of material" information is required, then CAD is clearly preferable over manual methods.

Similarly, a piece of work may conclude with a 3-dimensional visualization of the final image. This is one of CAD's fortes: a final visualization can rapidly be created from the data accrued during the project. There would be little point, therefore, in using manual methods, only to then have to recreate the work on CAD to construct the 3-D image.

Does the work involve the calculation of complex figures at any point? A CAD system can often provide data instantly that would be a nightmare for anyone to calculate using traditional methods — for instance, the length of a complex curve, the area of an irregular shape, or the volume of a peculiar solid.

Let's face it, nowadays almost any project is suited to CAD techniques. Limitations are more likely to be due to weaknesses in hardware, software, or staff—the three resources examined in Chapter 17.

When, for whatever reason, restrictions are placed on the amount of work that can be allocated to the CAD system, it is wise to concentrate on creating work that is of use to many departments. For example, architectural site plans, office floorplans, and so on can provide a common foundation for all design-related work throughout the project.

The Work Schedule

The job will suffer if CAD is not included in the workload plan. As I have mentioned already, considering the current and future workload commitments is necessary if CAD is to play a worthwhile role.

A work schedule is a formalized way of preventing the valuable CAD resource being wasted, by indicating who is doing what work, and when, and with what equipment.

Resources were already covered in Chapter 17, with the evaluation of capabilities such as personnel, software, and hardware. This chapter is concerned with ensuring the availability of these resources to complete the workload allocation.

A "here and now" approach to workload allocation will result in panic-driven management and a confused and irritated workforce. A "scheduled" approach, however, will prevent the conflict caused by projects and people competing for CAD time. Being able to predict partially into the future encourages the effective use of resources.

A well-planned workload is vital if potentially damaging problems are to be avoided. For instance, when a CAD designer is unable to get onto a computer, he has no option but to wait until the machine becomes available again; he cannot just continue his work on a drawing board.

When the demand for the CAD facility becomes overwhelming, an increase must be made in either the number of CAD workstations or the time spent working with them. The latter can be achieved by introducing a shift system, possibly continuing throughout the night with an overlap period to allow communication with the rest of the design team.

Staff having to share CAD terminals is a familiar source of discontent. Yet, even if a workstation is allocated to every designer in the company, unless they all spend 24 hours a day working at it, the system will be underutilized.

Workload representation

When considering whether to apportion workload to the CAD department the availability and suitability of the staff, software, and hardware needs to be considered.

By "availability" I am referring to the current and future commitments. That is, the number of resource units that are free and not free at any particular time. The "suitability" is the appropriateness of the resource unit for the job. This is something that should be evaluated as described previously in Chapter 17.

An often-forgotten aspect of the workload is the time and effort spent on tasks other than the actual job. For example, time and resources need to be allocated to backing up files and maintaining equipment. If these essential chores are not included with the workplan, they are not likely to be done, which would inevitably result in undesirable consequences.

All relevant information must be represented in a way that makes workload commitments easy to determine. In addition, a suitable schedule should provide up-to-date and accurate information on the following:

- details and duration of projects or elements of projects being worked on
- equipment being used and when it is being used
- which staff are working, when they are working, and what they are working on
- potential bottlenecks (such as during plotting)
- unproductive time to be spent on system customization, maintenance, etc.
- variations of CAD usage throughout projects (which often increases toward the end)
- workload priorities (a schedule may be redrafted to accommodate a priority job)

Presenting this information schematically with charts and histograms, rather than confusing tables of figures, allows a lot of facts to be conveyed in a clear and concise way. Work schedule information in this form can easily be assimilated.

The chart shown in Fig. 19-1 is a schedule taken from a company with four projects to be worked on over the forthcoming six months. They have thirty CAD workstations and thirty members of staff available to use them. Resources are allocated weekly, although other organizations may find it more appropriate to allocate them daily or even hourly.

When a schedule like this is tentatively put together, there is likely to be peaks and troughs of demand for resources. The schedule can then be redrafted to smooth them out as much as possible. In Fig. 19-1, see how Project 4 is delayed until Project 2 requires less resources. This task is made easier if at least one of the projects being worked on is flexible enough to be chopped and changed to fill any gaps between the other projects. Where an excess demand on resources occurs, the decision can be made how to deal with it. Maybe freelancers could be used, a system of shifts arranged, or work could be farmed out elsewhere.

Any changes occurring to the charts must be communicated to all concerned quickly. For this reason, computer-generated schedules are a good idea — and yet another possible use for CAD.

Workload overload

When the CAD workload is greater than can be coped with by existing resources, it does not mean that the scheduling system has failed, rather that it has succeeded in identifying this overload of work. In such circumstances, we are faced with two choices: either increase staff and equipment effectiveness, or send the work to be done outside of the office.

The second solution usually leads to a CAD/Design Bureau. Bureaus also provide a useful service to the many companies that wish to benefit from CAD techniques but do not want to have a system installed

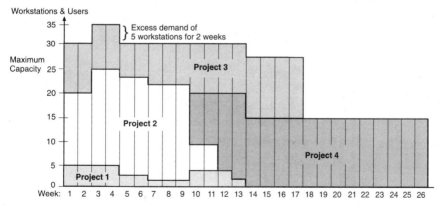

Figure 19-1 A schedule for CAD work.

in their own organization. They may feel like this because of the high cost, limited office space, or a lack of trained staff.

Instructing a bureau clearly on the job requirements and then leaving them to get on with it will take a piece of the overall workload out of a company's hands. Of course there is a cost, but the advantage of having the work done by CAD rather than on the drawing board may outweigh this.

What to Do

- Identify the elements of the work that are most suited to CAD techniques.
- Organize the current and future commitments of staff and equipment using accessible graphical work schedules where possible.

20

Drawing

A good CAD user spends time before the first line is drawn to consider the most suitable approach to take to the work ahead. This is one reason why CAD techniques often prove slower than traditional methods when creating completely new drawings. When not just a single drawing but a whole project is about to commence, initial thought and preparation given to drawing approach is even more worthwhile.

Problems can arise when many designers are working on the same project. Each one may have planned an approach to take — methods that are fine individually, but differ from each other. The chaos that can result will not arise if they all "play by the same rules" and work to the same drawing conventions. Standards and conventions in design work suit the regimented style of CAD more so than they do the less orderly traditional methods.

Whatever procedures are involved in tackling the work, ideas can only be conveyed to the world outside the office by the final images that are created. The impact of good work will be impaired by poor presentation. The presentation of these images is, therefore, a crucial concern.

Initial thoughts on the approach taken to drawing work will be developed when the CAD Manager is briefed, along with the Project Manager and others, on the job to be done. Much of the approach will be common to all projects and consequently already be in place.

The Merits of 2-D and 3-D

If, for example, a project involves office layouts, the scope of the work may seem to be restricted to flat plan views. However, think a bit harder. A 3-dimensional view of an image is nearly always worthwhile, either to replace 2-dimensional views or used in conjunction with them.

Unfortunately, most of us are all still conditioned to think with a 2-dimensional "paper" mentality. CAD allows us easy access to a

3-dimensional space that, though more like the real world, may not be so easy to cope with in our minds.

It is true that 2-dimensional plans interface better with existing office practices, but they convey no more information than a manual drawing. The only advantage over drawing manually is the availability of CAD tools to assist in its creation.

What is more, to read 2-dimensional engineering and many architectural drawings accurately requires a specialist knowledge. This alienates everyone without this talent. A great number of people, therefore, will be unable to comprehend the ideas the designer is attempting to convey.

An alternative approach to this is to create the image as a 3-dimensional "model" on the CAD system. This digitally formed model can be manipulated and analyzed using the 2-D, as well as special 3-D CAD commands.

The 3-D world offers many possibilities:

- *Wireframe modeling* consists of the outlines of the object. They can be used to convey most images and are relatively simple to use, though not so visually appealing. The skeletal appearance of wireframe models is often useful during the design process where being able to see through the image allows the designer greater insight.

- *Surface modeling* produces the effect of a fine mesh pulled tightly over the object to form an effect like a skin as opposed to the wireframe skeleton, allowing complex surfaces to be constructed. It is most suited to "organic" shapes, such as a horse's saddle or the curved panels of a car.

- *Solid modeling* is analogous to building a model with pieces of solid material. Boolean expressions to add and subtract one 3-D shape from another simplify the process. Although this form of 3-D work is most applicable when regular-shaped components are involved, complex components such as engine parts can be modeled as long as they can be created by combining simpler solids. An added advantage of solid modeling is the ease with which the object's properties (mass and so on) can be analyzed. Figure 20-1 shows an example of solid modeling created using AutoCAD Release 13.

- *Rendering* allows a 3-D image that has been created by either solid or surface modeling to be transformed by the application of light, color, and texture into a photo-realistic image. The potential of this capability will be limited by the sophistication of the CAD system, although many bureaus exist that will take a CAD image and render it out of the office.

3-D modeling requires a greater level of CAD skill from the designer. More thought will be needed prior to commencement, so it is slower to produce results.

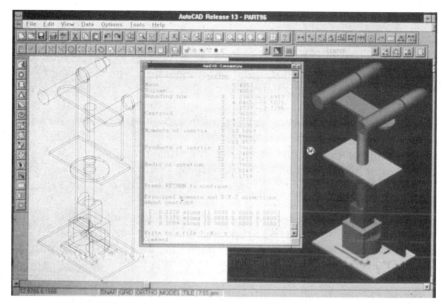

Figure 20-1. 3-dimensional solid modeling. *(Autodesk Ltd.)*

3-dimensional creations allow analysis and experimentation. For instance, volume, mass, manufacturing information, lighting effects, and so on can all be considered at the early stages of the design processes, as if the design being worked on had really been created. This is a better use of the CAD facility than the "flat" approach as it offers something way beyond drafting — a virtual reality.

Although the larger drawing files can become quite cumbersome, a drawing including a combination of 2-D and 3-D images will convey more information and be easier for a person unskilled in the reading of technical drawings to comprehend.

There is a halfway house — the so-called "2½ dimension"— where 2-D images are displayed in 3-D space. Simple structures, such as a cube and sphere, from a library of predefined 3-D primitives may also be included.

A common application of "2½-D" are locational diagrams of multistory buildings. The 2-D images of each floor can be displayed in their respective levels and viewed in 3-D perspective.

Going back to the initial example, would an office layout not benefit from some 3-D imagery? Maybe an axonometric overview and a selection of views taken from specific places in the plan, possibly including the view one sees when entering through the door or when sitting at a particular desk.

The rare occasions where it may be sufficient to stick to only 2-D images is in work that involves a purely 2-D environment, such as electronic circuit board layouts.

Setting Drawing Standards

Standards are important in any professional organization and are the essence of quality in the design office. They display clarity, conformity, and coherence between individual designers throughout a project. The opportunity to standardize elements of design work is an advantage of the CAD facility over manual methods that must be exploited.

In addition to the existing drawing office standards, CAD offers others of its own. Layering, for instance, is a powerful way of regulating and standardizing output. Similarly, the wide range of text styles on offer presents possibilities beyond anything achievable manually. Vast libraries of drawing elements can be accumulated, possibly sampled from past projects or purchased en masse.

As with most of the procedures mentioned in this part of the book, it is worthwhile confirming the principles that are to govern the drawing approach before work commences. There are two ways of accomplishing this:

- Document all standards and present them to the designers with an instruction to implement them.

- Customize the CAD system to automatically incorporate the principles in a series of prototype drawings. The designer will then find many of the standards — text styles, dimension styles, layers, and so on — already in place when a drawing is begun. The method is clearly preferable to the first.

Prototype drawings

A great deal of information other than the actual drawing data is stored in the CAD drawing file. As well as the factory set defaults, there are settings defined by the user that relate to a particular drawing.

The initial environment facing a designer when a new drawing is begun is the canvas on which the design is created. It is possible to customize the CAD system to define a personalized initial environment — in other words, to prepare in advance the starting point from which a new drawing can be developed. In fact, it is possible to create a variety of prototypes providing numerous initial starting points from which the designer can choose.

During the discussion that follows on presetting standards using prototype drawings the technical terms and techniques I use relate to "AutoCAD" — the most popular CAD software in the world. Even so, the principles discussed also apply to most other CAD packages.

The default drawing The initial environment present when a new drawing file is opened is itself a drawing. The name of this initial drawing is held within the system's configuration data. If no drawing name has been specified in the configuration data, a factory set default drawing called ACAD.DWG is automatically used.

This may be changed to a drawing name specified by the user by selecting the "Initial drawing setup" option from the Configuration menu. This will prompt for the name of the default drawing. Any drawing name can be entered. For example, if

\DRAWINGS\PROTO

is entered and a drawing called PROTO exists in the \DRAWINGS directory, it will from then on define the initial environment for any forthcoming new drawings. This method permanently alters the system's default prototype so care must be taken on multiuser CAD systems.

Overriding the default drawing An alternative to the previous method is to create a one-off deviation from the normal prototype by overriding it when entering the drawing editor.

When specifying the name of a new drawing an initial template can be requested by adding an "=" followed by the name of the desired prototype. For example:

Enter name of drawing: PLAN1=PLAN

This would open a drawing called PLAN1 that is identical to another drawing called PLAN. This prototype may contain all the prerequisite elements needed for any plan drawings.

It is a good idea to give prototype drawings clear recognizable names (ELEV for elevations, for instance) so that they can be accessed without having to search for the appropriate file.

The empty default drawing Occasionally it is useful to begin a new drawing without any predefined prototype — to have as blank a canvas as is possible. To create this, just add an equal sign after the new drawing name:

Enter name of drawing: OFFICE=

A drawing named OFFICE would be created with an environment defined by the most basic settings of the AutoCAD software.

When to use prototype drawings Customized prototypes are particularly useful when a company is working on numerous long-term projects simultaneously. Designers will find it beneficial to have at least one prototype drawing for each project available as a foundation on which to construct their work.

For example, consider a company specializing in three types of work: store plans, electrical diagrams, and space planning. A separate directory called \PROTO\ could be created to hold the corresponding prototypes, STORE, ELEC, and PLAN. The relevant prototype drawing can then be accessed using the "new name=prototype name" method. So, for example, work on a new store plan called NEWSTORE would begin by entering

NEWSTORE=\PROTO\STORE

As well as this, a general prototype could be specified in the configuration data to be used when a drawing requires neither of the three prototypes. This would be accessed using the "new name" only method:

NEWSTORE

Finally, if neither of these methods are suitable, the "new name=" option would access the most basic default as the prototype:

NEWSTORE=

What can be included in a prototype drawing?

Whatever the name of the prototype drawing, and however it is accessed, the reason for using it is to implant information to be there when needed. This information, such as text styles and dimension units, can be printed out and made available to the design team, allowing it to be examined away from the CAD terminal. Elements of it may also be incorporated in the Project file and in the company's Quality Assurance documentation.

Here are some suggestions on what may be useful for a designer to have preset in a prototype drawing.

Drawing elements Include elements that regularly appear throughout the project. Remember that this information will increase the time to enter and regenerate a drawing, so do not get carried away with it. In some cases, such as a complex title block, it would be preferable instead to insert it last of all, when the drawing has been completed.

Blocks Insert commonly used Blocks (permanently grouped drawing elements) into the prototype, then erase them. This means that, although the Blocks are not visible in the new drawing, they are held in its memory and can be readily listed and accessed by the designer.

Layers Define the name, status (thawed/frozen, on/off), color, and linetype of each layer. Set to the layer that is required to be current at the start of new drawings. For the sake of clarity, remember that the order in which layer names are defined is the same order that they will appear on the layer list.

Text styles Define the name, font, height, width factor, and so on of any number of text styles. It is worthwhile giving them appropriate names — such as Title, Rooms, and Notes — in a floor plan as way of indicating their use.

Units Set the precision of linear and angular units and decide which format to use for their display. These settings may be determined by the conventions of the country that the drawing is destined for.

Views Viewpoints can be defined to "look" at specific areas. With 3-dimensional work, for instance, it may be advantageous to divide the screen into four views to display the plan, front elevation, side elevation, and 3-D isometric as shown in Figure 20-2.

Menu All CAD commands can be accessed via a command menu. Alternative menus can be created for specific situations. A specially created menu may contain functions customized to fulfill the requirements for a particular project. If, for example, work switches from a product design job to an architectural job, a prototype drawing would be used that contains a menu that simplifies access to architectural functions and symbols.

Dimensioning variables Dimensions appear in a style determined by the values assigned to numerous dimensioning variables. The full list and meaning of each one will be explained in the software's Reference Manual. The number and complexity of these variables makes it difficult to alter them "on the hoof"; presetting them in the prototype drawing is certainly worthwhile.

System variables Alter the values of system variables to determine many of the factors that define the working environment. Some are simple on/off toggles, while others are more versatile. For example, shown in Fig. 20-3 are a few of AutoCAD's system variables and their initial values as set in ACAD.DWG, the default prototype.

Drawing Presentation

As CAD systems have evolved over recent years, the opportunity for individual flair has increased. At the same time, the sight of a drawing

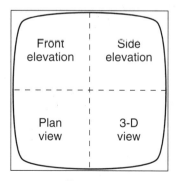

Figure 20-2. Preset viewpoints.

VARIABLE NAME	MEANING	VALUE
AXISMODE	axis display	0 (off)
BLIPMODE	marker blips display	1 (on)
COORDS	coordinate display	0 (picks only)
DRAGMODE	dragged image visibility	2 (auto)
FILLETRAD	fillet radius	0.0
GRIDMODE	grid function	0 (off)
LTSCALE	linetype scale factor	1
MENUECHO	prompts for visibility	0 (all)
MIRRTEXT	mirrored text	1 (reflects text)
ORTHOMODE	orthographic drawing mode	0 (off)
QTEXTMODE	simplified text while drawing	0 (off)
REGENMODE	automatic regeneration of image	1 (on)
SNAPANG	snap/grid rotation	0.0
SNAPMODE	snap function	0 (off)
UCSICON	coordinate icon visibility	1 (on)

Figure 20-3. Some of Autocad's default System Variables.

created with a computer is no longer sufficient to draw automatic praise. As well as the distinction between CAD and manual techniques, there is now a distinction made between well-presented CAD drawings and those that are poorly presented.

Presentation criteria overlaps with the previously discussed topic of drawing standards and similarly, prototype drawings are a good, reliable way of enforcing them. These presentation criteria determine the final appearance of the work. It becomes a matter of pride when the work, as well as being technically flawless, has the appearance of a piece of fine art.

The three major elements of a technical drawing — lines, text, and dimensions — can vary greatly according to individual style.

Line thickness may either be created within the drawing or by the output device, usually a plotter. The latter is preferable as it allows greater flexibility.

The commonly available plotter pen thicknesses are 0.25mm, 0.35mm, 0.5mm, and 0.7mm. If the outer walls of an architectural drawing, for example, are to appear thicker than the rest of the drawing, they can be drawn in a different color on the computer screen (say, red). Then the red color can be assigned to a thicker pen than the other colors in the drawing. If subsequently the same drawing is printed onto A4 paper to be faxed, all lines will need to be thin to aid clarity. To accomplish this, the drawing need not be altered, just the pen assignments in the plot routine.

Text styles can be selected from the large choice available in the basic CAD package or from additional "add-on" fonts that can be purchased. The range of text styles is enormous. Some, ironically, have the appearance of handwritten text.

Text that accompanies dimensions should correspond to other text notes used throughout the drawing.

Seasoned CAD designers use the most basic and unappealing text fonts during the design process. This is to keep the time spent regenerating the image on the screen during work down to a minimum. A more appealing style is substituted at the end of the work using a simple procedure.

It is true that dimension style conventions differ according to the drawing's subject matter: architectural, engineering, and so on. However, in any drawing, a little forethought can result in clearer and presentable dimensioning.

What to Do

- The CAD Manager, the Project Manager, and possibly others should decide the approach to be taken to all drawing work.

- The CAD user should spend time in preparation before the first line is drawn. This preparation will increase if the drawing approach involves 3-dimensional work.

- Utilize the 3-dimensional facilities for drawing and viewing the design.

- Use drawing standards to display clarity, conformity, and coherence between individual designers throughout a project.

- Where possible, preset these standards in prototype drawings.

- Exploit the possibilities of text, lineweight, dimensions, and so on. There are plenty of opportunities for individual style to show in a drawing.

Output

The output, in whatever form, is the finished product of the whole CAD design process. It will communicate the ideas that have been generated during the creative stages and provide the most tangible evidence of the success or otherwise of the CAD facility. As well as its normal function, therefore, CAD output is open to judgmental scrutiny.

This output will not necessarily consist only of paper plots but can take many forms. For example, data may leave the design office via a modem line to be used as input for a lithographer. Generally speaking, the output falls into two categories:

- *Paper:* Plots from a pen, electrostatic, or laser plotter.
- *Electronic:* Data in various filetypes (DWG, DXF, SLD, etc.) stored and transmitted using disk, tape, modem, etc.

A CAD file is not simply a drawing; the information it contains may be used to create a variety of output. In other words, its content can be tailored to the requirements of the client by altering such parameters as the layer status and the viewpoint. Because of this, many different paper drawings can be plotted from a single CAD drawing.

Whatever the particular form and content of the output, it must conform to the drawing office style and standards. Among other things, this means having all output checked by a suitably qualified person. This process is represented schematically in Fig. 21-1.

Ongoing Appraisal

Throughout the drawing process there will inevitably be a number of dimensional inaccuracies, drawing errors, technical faults, misprints, changes in the project brief, and so on. Because of this, reworking will always be necessary, despite CAD's acclaimed accuracy. The amount of

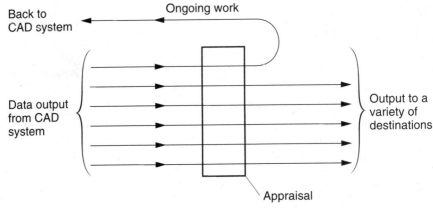

Figure 21-1. All output from CAD system must be appraised.

reworking will be reduced if in-house checks are made on all output occurring throughout the project as well as on the final issue.

As the latest accurate drawings are produced, they should be duplicated and reissued to the relevant departments throughout the company. This will ensure that the whole design team is working to the same plan. For the same reason, it is wise to discard any superseded output.

In the case of paper plots, the most likely form of output at this stage, the layer status, plotter settings, pen thickness, pen color, and so on, are almost as important as the data contained in the drawing. Failing to have these parameters correctly set will result in a misleading representation of the work.

Bear in mind also the accuracy of the plotter, or any other output device, for that matter. There is no advantage in having a CAD system performing with 100% accuracy if the output is produced using a 95% accurate plotter. It is sensible to perform regular checks on the accuracy of output devices if this sort of situation is to be avoided.

During the course of their work, CAD designers may wish to use paper plots of their drawings for analysis away from the computer. Consequently, when any checking procedure is implemented, it is important to distinguish between the intermediate test-plots and the final drawing.

Problems can arise also when moving data around an office electronically, such as identifying current work from old, having data be incomplete, and having incompatibility between differing systems. As new technology is introduced into the office, awareness of potential trouble areas is vital.

The key to appraisal is checking. The person, or people, with responsibility for checking must view all output. It is possible to use the CAD system as a viewing facility simply to review existing CAD drawings. That is, images can rapidly be displayed on-screen, avoiding the need to rummage through piles of paper drawings. In fact, there is no need to tie up a powerful CAD machine to do this. If the checker is only annotating the drawings with correction notes, a simpler graphics machine may be used instead. The annotations will be present on the drawing when the designer begins work again at the CAD terminal where the corrections will be made.

Completed Work

The task faced by the person, or people, nominated to independently verify work prior to its issue may involve simply looking over the drawings very carefully or performing a set of relevant test calculations.

The primary source of error will be dimensional inaccuracies. Although CAD's dimensioning facility is perfectly accurate there is still the possibility of a designer's error, such as misreading or mistyping a figure. A degree of human error is also inherent in the checking. As a safeguard, it is wise to include a note in the title block disclaiming responsibility for the accuracy of information contained in the drawing.

There are other things to check for. For example, checks need to be made for the correct application of drawing standards as outlined in Chapter 20.

For both paper or electronic output, the form and quality of the media must be considered. So, when output takes the form of electronic data (disk, tape, modem transmissions, and so on) it must be reliably durable and its data must be clarified with accompanying information such as fonts, printouts, and listings.

As far as is possible, the traceability of output must be maintained, that is, "who sent what where and when?" should be detailed in the company's receipt and issue records. In practice this is rarely tackled properly, but when Quality Assurance procedures exist in the company, it is a matter that must be addressed.

What to Do

- Use in-house checking of all CAD output, not just the final issue, to minimize error and reworking.

- Achieve this by nominating a checker to either look over the drawing very carefully or perform a set of relevant test calculations on the work.

Project Planning

Most of us have experienced that eleventh-hour panic where the only way to keep to the agreed deadline is to work all day, all night, and all weekend. Oddly, this has become the accepted way of working in many offices, as if it were an unavoidable consequence of working in the design industry.

This is ridiculous. The need to work extra hours as a matter of course just to get the job done is a reflection of poor management. More specifically, it is a result of unrealistic expectations and insufficient planning.

In the previous part of the book, I looked in some detail at the broad range of issues involved when the workload is tackled on the CAD system. Now I will look at how an individual project can pass peaceably through the modern design office, free from the sort of problems mentioned above.

A well-thought-out, orderly approach must be taken to a project from beginning to end to ensure its successful progression. This may be accomplished with the help of project management software. Such planning is vital if error-ridden work is to be avoided. Thinking things through before a project begins will dramatically cut wasted time, effort, and resources, as well as prevent numerous headaches.

22

A Route Plan for CAD Projects

For some reason, design departments frequently abandon tried and tested working practices when computers replace drawing boards. This may be because computers, being computers, are assumed to relieve humans of all responsibility and take such concerns out of their hands. This is obviously wrong, however, as projects performed using computer-aided design techniques are just as much in need of planning as those done on the drawing board. Project planning is part of the design process however the work is to be accomplished, and CAD must not be used as an excuse to abdicate responsibility.

Successful working practices, whatever production methods exist, will follow a planned course of action from start to finish, rather than a chaotic free-for-all. Such plans may not always be formalized and documented, but recognized procedures will always be followed so that the margin of error is minimized.

Design technology often unfairly receives the blame for the sort of troubles that inevitably occur when a project has not been properly planned. For instance, drawings lost due to confused naming systems are not the fault of CAD but are a result of poor project management. The CAD Manager and the CAD department can only be expected to take responsibility for CAD, not for the inadequate planning of the project as a whole which is the responsibility of the Project Manager.

The Project Manager

The responsibilities of the Project Manager encompass every aspect of the project. They must be just as dedicated to overseeing the CAD elements of the work as they are to overseeing the non-CAD elements of the work. They provide a link across all disciplines involved in the project and maintain continuity from the start of the project to its conclusion.

In Part 1 of this book (Management), a recurring problem was the senior person in a company who is only familiar with managing the passage of traditionally created drawings through the design office. Such a person will have been raised on the concept that a project progresses as the designer untapes a completed drawing from the drawing board and replaces it with a new, blank piece of paper ready to begin the next. In this situation, the work process is acted out in front of the Project Manager's eyes. All that need be done to assess the current state of the project is to look over the drafter's shoulder.

Things are very different in the CAD drawing office. The most obvious difference is that the developments in the project can take place very quickly and in the form of invisible data stored inside a computer. The need for order and management is more vital than ever.

For instance, rather than commencing with a blank sheet of paper, the starting point for a CAD designer may be derived from a combination of any number of data sources often imported directly into the CAD system. This initial jumble of data means that even the most orderly of designers can find themselves faced with drawings consisting of lines that do not meet where they should, inconsistent scales, varying text styles, and so on — and this is before the project has properly got underway!

In today's design office the task of the Project Manager must involve issues that were previously thought of as only concerning specialists such as rapid design development, instantaneous and far-reaching communications, data management, and so on. Consequently the subject of project management in the design office is a bigger and more complex one than ever before. It involves steering the work safely through all the CAD workload management issues discussed in Part 6 of this book.

What if the Project Manager is not able to contend with CAD issues? In such a situation, the CAD Manager must ensure that the problem is seen to lie with the Project Manager and not with CAD. It is unfortunately common for the CAD element of a project to be left to look after itself while the rest of the project is guided by the helpful hand of the Project Manager. Allowing this to happen will only result in the sidelining of CAD. As said at the beginning of this passage, the Project Manager must manage all of the project, not just the drawing board bit. Inevitably, at this point in time, this will involve cooperation with the CAD Manager, as indicated in Fig. 22-1.

The Project Plan

The full extent of a project comprises many stages during its progression from initial market enquiry to delivery of the final product. Figure 22-2 shows this and indicates the phase that involves predominantly CAD in this overall context.

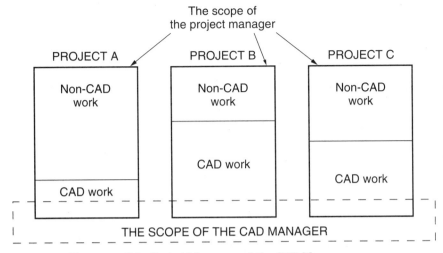

Figure 22-1. The scope of the Project Manager and the CAD Manager.

Successful management of the CAD workload was shown in Part 6 to comprise many issues which were examined by grouping them into six distinct areas:

- *Input:* Appraisal of raw materials
- *Resources:* Evaluation of personnel, software, and hardware
- *Data:* Protection of CAD data integrity
- *Scheduling:* Identification and organization of CAD work
- *Drawing:* Drawing standards and presentation
- *Output:* Conclusion of the CAD design process

A particular project will encounter each of these six areas during its time in the CAD office. Consider the project plan to be one of an infinite number of possible routes taking the design team through the issues, problems, and concerns included under these six headings. A successful route should pass through each area, covering any ground necessary for that particular project as represented in Fig. 22-3.

Long-established drawing offices, still using manual techniques, will have ways of dealing with work that have evolved over many years. Often there will be little change involved in applying these methods to the CAD drawing office. For example, the appraisal of input data is certainly not a new procedure that must be mastered when CAD enters the office but is a commonsense practice equally necessary in any drawing office, whether manual or computerized.

Similarly, drawing revisions have existed as long as drawing itself, with the only difference now being that drawings can be revised "on the hoof." It does not take long before numerous versions of a drawing

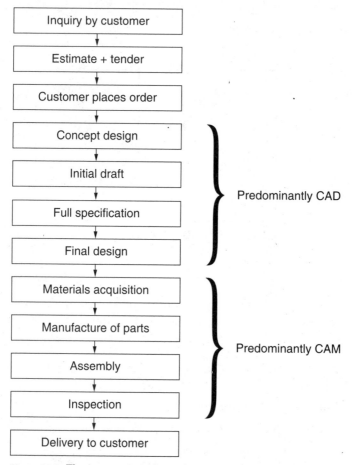

Figure 22-2. The progression of a project.

can exist at the same time. Therefore, an orderly system of creating, naming, and distributing revised work is essential to prevent it causing serious harm.

The ease of drawing creation can mean that, not long into a project, the hard disk can become choked with data. Consequently, the project's store of data needs to be managed. Questions such as "What work needs to be archived, when and where is it held?" should be answered in the project plan.

Remember, project planning is nothing new but just needs to be adapted to take in the concerns of the CAD environment. It is true that in many cases this has made project planning a "bigger" job than previously, but then CAD has made the activities of the design office "bigger."

Rather than boring you with specific project details taken from the contents of actual project files, this text will indicate some of the common areas of concern that must be resolved by the project management team prior to embarking on the journey, indicated in Fig. 22-3. If you were about to commence on a long car journey, you would very sensibly plan ahead by assessing the route to be taken and checking the car's resources — gas, oil, and water. Similarly, if the following points are not considered prior to the commencement of work, they can become major trouble spots later on in the project:

- *Examination of the potential workload.* Will the project involve work that is most suited to CAD or to manual techniques?

- *Analysis of up-to-date workload schedules.* Will the various resources that are needed for the project be free from other commitments?

- *Assessment of the staffing situation.* Are existing skill levels appropriate; if not, is training a viable option?

- *Evaluation of software and hardware resources.* Will existing capabilities be sufficient to cope with the work?

- *Development of procedures.* Are suitable procedures in place to deal with breakdown recovery, data security, drawing file management, and so on?

- *Implementation of drawing standards.* Are the entire design team singing from the same songsheet? That is, are one designer's standards and conventions the same as another's?

- *Definition of drawing style.* Is there a house, or project, style to be adhered to?

- *Appraisal of initial data.* Can all the different forms of source data be guaranteed to be free of inaccuracies and inconsistencies?

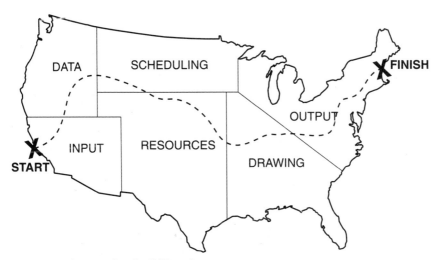

Figure 22-3. A route plan for CAD projects.

- *Continuous appraisal of input and output data.* How can the continual flow of data in and out of the CAD system be checked for inaccuracies?

- *Checking of the finished product.* How will work be assessed to ensure that the desired specifications are being met?

What to Do

- When computerization has taken place, build on the project planning procedures learned from the manual design environment.

- Define the scope of the Project Manager's activities.

- Follow a comprehensive plan for each project, from start to end.

- Follow a comprehensive plan for the CAD design phase, from input of data to output of finished product.

23

Project Management Software

All sorts of software packages like to consider themselves as aids for the running of projects, coming under a variety of labels — such as "office management," "CAD management," and "project planning" — and they all offer a similar but different facility. Some may focus on document management, some may be based around the CAD drawing database, and others may simply consist of a computerized card index built up by the user.

The software covered in this chapter — referred to as "project management software" — is a database application that provides a framework within which the project can progress, while constantly monitoring performance.

The previous chapter described the importance of planning projects. How well can software brought into the office accomplish this?

An Aid to Project Planning

For every CAD user involved in a project, numerous others want access to the CAD drawings and documentation. Project management software can straddle this projectwide demand. It will examine what is being done, by whom, and by when. The results of this can be collated and issued as reports, or utilized further, such as interfacing with company accounting systems.

It can be all things to all people. The Project Manager may use the package to examine how the work agenda is progressing, the CAD Manager will benefit from the opportunity to supervise without interfering with work, while the CAD designer may exploit the user-friendly file-finding and viewing facilities.

Most project management software packages tackle the procedural elements of project planning such as filenaming. The company's policy on this could be permanently incorporated into the system so that the user has no choice but to comply.

Contrary to what many people think, this kind of software does not replace the need for a project plan. If it is used, it is only as a tool to assist planning. The package that offers the most features is not necessarily the best one for your company; the most suitable is the one that helps to fulfill the company's project planning criteria.

What Does Project Management Software Offer?

It is often presumed that all project management software packages offer the same basic facilities. A little forethought, however, will ensure that a package suited to the user's particular needs is purchased. Covered here are many of the features offered by the project management software packages available today.

User control Every person accessing the CAD database should have to log in and then out once finished. Simultaneous access by more than one user provides for multiuser CAD systems.

The rights of access to the data can differ according to circumstances. For instance, the person checking the drawings for errors may be allowed to plot out work but not to edit drawings, while the designers could be given sufficient access to enable them to edit drawings but not to delete or rename them. This sort of access control is a valuable security device.

The results of this monitoring can be presented in the form of a report. This provides details mainly on time usage such as, who did what and when, the time spent unproductively or the time spent plotting, among other things.

Software interface The poor interface between the operator and their design tool is often stated as a disadvantage of CAD. A good, well-thought-out interface is a valuable part of any project management software.

A feature commonly found is the file previewing and selection facility. In most standard CAD packages the front end (the "way in") is unwieldy to say the least. The ability to flit from file to file, viewing as you go, before selecting the desired drawing file, is an undoubted boon for users.

In an equally simple and straightforward way, all the details normally recorded in the title box can be input to a user interface that will request everything from the day's date to revision details. These facts will then be automatically placed in the title box and simultaneously recorded in the software's database.

Data interchange Compatibility with other databases will allow information exchanges to take place. If the software is independent of the CAD system it operates on, then it will likely be able to access and receive input from a wider range of sources throughout the office.

Database housekeeping This entails keeping track of all data files, whether they are in progress, completed, or to be removed.

A useful utility incorporated into some software is an automatic backup and archiving procedure. For example, it may be set to do a full system and drawing backup at midnight every Sunday, and an incremental drawing backup at midnight every night.

Data integrity This is a measure of the reliability of the information coming out from the CAD system. For instance, good data integrity requires the ability to recover from a user "crashing out" of a piece of work, mid-drawing, without leaving remnants of the file scattered throughout the hard disk. Most eventualities will be catered for, but beware because nothing is foolproof. The opportunity to manually access the system's database and correct any errors is still a worthwhile option.

What to Do

■ Use project management software as a tool to aid the project planning procedures discussed in Chapter 22.

■ Select the project management software package carefully to meet the needs of the individual company and project.

8

Quality Assurance (QA)

So far in this book, I have written a lot about the practices and procedures that allow CAD to be applied effectively in a company.

Throughout all areas of business Quality Assurance (QA) is regarded as a way to keep every individual and every department focused and efficient. What happens when this modern business practice comes into contact with modern design methods?

Quality Assurance is common sense written down. Persevere with it and the result will be a working practice free of the self-induced crises common in many design offices.

In this part of the book, I describe how Quality Assurance procedures are applicable to design technology and explain with the aid of examples the documentation necessary to implement a QA system in a CAD department.

I should stress that this part of the book is essential reading whether your company intends to be officially accredited with a QA standard or not. The clarification of aims, procedures, and responsibilities is an asset for any organization or individual employee.

24

QA and CAD

The rewards of a recognizably successful policy that seeks to guarantee not only a product's quality but the quality of the whole production and management process is one surely worth pursuing, whether or not one intends to be officially accredited with a QA standard or not.

Following recognizable professional standards of some description is nothing new. For instance, educational qualifications are demanded of most new recruits to guarantee a certain standard of knowledge, and multinational standards are agreed to ensure compatibility and accessibility to the maximum number of customers.

The QA standard is not simply a measure of a product's quality but of the company's management system.

Quality Assurance has it roots in General MacArthur's mission to rebuild Japan's manufacturing base after it had been irradicated by allied bombs in World War II. As part of his plans, MacArthur arranged for Japanese engineering students to be trained at American colleges. Here they came into contact with the philosophy of Quality as pioneered by Dr. W. Deming. His message proved so popular with the Japanese students that he was later invited to Japan to lecture. The industrial giants that we know today — Nissan, Mitsubishi, Sony, and hundreds of other companies — were all eager to learn from Deming. While these seeds were being sown in the East, Western industry paid no serious attention to Deming's philosophy. Now, 50 years after suffering a devastating defeat, Japan's working practices have proved so successful that they are now one of the world's leading economic powers.

In the UK, Quality Assurance first made footholds in the defense industry. Companies involved with defense work were audited according to the MoD's own quality assurance system. These companies were often at the core of British manufacturing, so the concept of quality assurance soon became known.

"Quality" is a word often used subjectively in business parlance. However, there is in existence an objective quality standard, and what is actually required to attain this standard is laid down by the international standard ISO 9000. This standard—and others, such as the British BS 5750 and the European EN 29000—were harmonized in 1987 and are sometimes referred to as BS EN ISO 9000. A company conforming to BS 5750 will, therefore, be recognized both internationally and nationally.

Let us clarify things with a few definitions taken from ISO 8402-1986:

Quality: The total features and characteristics of a product or service that bear on its ability to satisfy stated or implied needs.

Quality Assurance: All those planned and systematic actions necessary to provide adequate confidence that a product or service will satisfy given requirements for quality.

Quality Control: The operational techniques and activities that are used to fulfill requirements for quality.

Quality Policy: The overall quality intentions and direction of an organization as regards quality, as formally expressed by top management.

Quality Management: That aspect of the overall management function that determines and implements the quality policy.

Quality System: The organizational structure, responsibilities, procedures, processes, and resources for implementing quality management.

Everybody's Doing It

Over the last three decades, consumers' awareness of quality has gradually increased, and they have a good idea of which companies guarantee the standards required by QA. Organizations unsure of whether or not to commit to QA are now being led by their consumers' preferences.

Originally written for manufacturing industries, ISO 9000 is relevant to any business. As far as design is concerned, the Design Council has stated that it considers this standard to be beneficial to the design industry. At the moment, relatively few service industries are officially registered for quality assurance, but the signs are that this is definitely changing. QA accreditation is confidently predicted to be commonplace throughout all sectors of business in a matter of a few years.

One influencing factor in the UK is the decision by all UK government departments to give suppliers with QA accreditation priority over those suppliers without it.

One of the implicit tenets of ISO 9000 is to use suppliers also accredited. Therefore, whether liked or loathed, it is inevitably going to spread through all companies, services, and manufacturing at an increasing rate.

Potential clients abroad, especially Japan, that are already converted to the QA system are naturally concerned at the level of quality at many of their suppliers.

More and more design consultancies are pursuing ISO 9000 certification. This can only be to their advantage when pitching for work against nonaccredited agencies.

There is a belief that states that QA and similar working practices belong to the Japanese and German workplaces and are an anathema to the "old" economies, as if it were a cultural difference. This is clearly not true. The fact is that these countries took QA to their hearts, while the rest of the world held back. The results of their forward thinking is obvious. Any cultural differences that do occur are between companies rather than countries.

There is no point in moaning about how it is more trouble than it is worth or how QA is irrelevant to your company. QA has clear benefits, and more and more companies are realizing this and following suit. It might seem a chore initially, but QA does make work easier in the medium and long term. So, to borrow a phrase from Nike, don't philosophize about it: just do it.

The QA Process

Implementing and being awarded the ISO 9000 certificate can take 18 months or so, though the actual necessary time depends largely on the resources committed to the task. The process involves four basic stages, and Fig. 24-1 indicates how these stages relate to the CAD department.

Stage 1: The Policy Manual

A QA consultant will be brought in early on in the QA process, and without her expert advice, the task is almost impossible. She will help the company develop a Policy Manual, which contains the company's quality intentions, management responsibility, operating procedures, and how the standard is applied to the company's particular field of work.

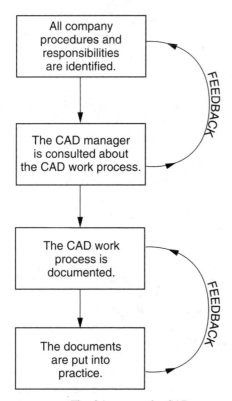

Figure 24-1. The QA process for CAD.

Stage 2: Companywide discussion

Next follows discussions with representatives from the whole of the company, the CAD Manager obviously being an important contributor.

Stage 3: Documentation

All processes, procedures, responsibilities, and resources for implementing what is outlined in the Policy Manual are described in a series of Quality Manuals and Documents. These are discussed more fully later in the book. Every area of the company's QA policy will be covered by a separate document, prepared by the company's staff with the assistance of the QA consultant. Specialized areas, such as CAD, will be written by the CAD Manager.

A test of the policy's effectiveness is if the company is able to continue working, untroubled, when a member of staff is not present. The business must be stronger than any individual and so should carry on as usual, whoever is missing. (Humorously, this is the "What if Mr. X was hit by a bus?" test.)

Stage 4: Feedback

Once the system is up and running, a continuous process of adjustment takes place; the QA documentation is not set in stone.

Numerous feedback loops are present in the overall QA system. For example, then, a designer will be aware of the concerns and requirements of the manufacturer and the customer. The designer is directly involved in the planning, testing, and reviewing of the product. Similarly the designer's original brief will be the result of research to ensure that it is known exactly what the task is and that this is exactly what is required by the customer. There should be no room for misunderstandings.

QA Practices in a CAD Environment

Senior management at numerous companies must have sat through seminars on QA, read the magazine articles, and seen its effectiveness in other companies, and then thought that, as terrific as it may be, it does not seem applicable to their own situation.

It is important to see beyond the QA jargon and procedures and grasp the basic concept of QA: common sense. The design industry has only recently become aware of QA and is discovering that it can change the whole culture of a company for the better. Persevere with it, and the result will be a working practice free of most of the self-induced crises that plague many design offices. It should mean the end to the "short-termism" and "firefighting" all too prevalent in the design business.

As far as the CAD industry is concerned, QA has been present right from the beginning. As QA certification spreads throughout all business sectors, CAD suppliers and developers wanting to introduce their products to these sectors realize that they must also meet the same standard.

Computers demand organization and so often lead the way in a company's QA policy. In fact, many would say that their sole reason for introducing CAD into the drawing office is to enhance the quality of their working methods.

CAD itself does not get much of a mention in the ISO 9000 compendiums, although the value of CAD is apparent when terms such as "periodic evaluation of the design" and "unambiguous documentation" are mentioned. This book previously mentions how the capabilities of CAD reduce the time and effort involved in QA feedback loops and how a person unfamiliar with engineering drawings is more able to understand the designer's intent when CAD 3-D and 2-D images are used.

The effect on working practices is very noticeable. Clients will receive a product that is right the first time, and as efficiency increases, time and resources will be saved, which results in decreased costs.

The numerous documents that comprise the QA system are prepared by the company's staff. The CAD Manager, being in such an influential position (see Chapter 2), will play a key part and may well be the driving force behind it all.

Many designers have a romantic vision of themselves working purely within the confines of their own imagination, isolated from the realities of the manufacturing process that inevitably follows design work. This is unrealistic. QA ensures that the product being designed meets the requirements of the customer. This gives rise to the most frequently heard complaint from the design team: "All this QA stuff will get in the way of our creativity." This is not true: QA will not hinder the creative process but improve it. Everyone in the company will be playing by the same rules, each individual being allowed to fulfill their job requirements within a well-defined framework. So the "creators" can concentrate on what they do best — being creative — while other departments in the company are taking good care of their own particular duties.

It is true that some companies use the QA label as a marketing tool without actually implementing it. However, when properly installed, QA policy significantly enhances the CAD workplace, allowing the workers to do what they do, knowing that they will not have their efforts thwarted by inefficiencies and mismanagement.

This part of the book does not offer a comprehensive discussion on QA. It covers all areas involving CAD and the CAD department. It is assumed that the CAD QA system would form part of the overall QA plan for the company. Of course, if your company is not and does not intend to pursue QA accreditation, then there is certainly no harm done in following these guidelines for the CAD department alone. As mentioned earlier, it is usually one department that leads the way in QA, so it may as well be CAD.

To reiterate this important point: everything discussed in this part of the book constitutes good CAD management, and I would suggest very strongly that the documentation and procedures mentioned in the following three chapters should form a permanent part of the CAD departments working practice, "whether or not the company has an official QA policy." QA practices applied to a CAD environment simply make very good sense.

What to Do

- Work to Quality Assurance standards in the CAD department whether or not your company is pursuing official accreditation.

- Remember, the QA standard is not simply a measure of the quality of the product but of the company's management system.

- Implement QA in four stages:

  1. Produce a Policy Manual with the assistance of a QA consultant.
  2. Discuss it with all areas of the company.
  3. Document all processes, procedures, responsibilities, and resources.
  4. Constantly modify policy using feedback mechanisms.

25

Preparing CAD QA Policy

The one thing guaranteed to make people flinch when they discuss QA is the preparatory work it involves. The thought of a never-ending circle of memos, meetings, studies, documentation and more documentation is enough to put anyone off. Fortunately it need not be that way. In this chapter I will show how straightforward it is to create a QA policy for a CAD facility. I will look first at personal responsibilities and then the necessary documentation.

Defining Responsibilities

It is essential that everyone in the company should know where responsibility lies throughout the whole design process.

The workload involved in QA preparation is tackled by a combination of a number of people—normally including Project Managers, the CAD Manager, and the design team. These people should decide for each stage of the work process who shall be responsible for:

- coordinating input
- monitoring ongoing work
- approving work at predetermined stages
- deciding whether work will continue or change direction
- coordinating output

For each of these, we need to know how and when they are tackled and the documentation required to put it "on the record."

There will inevitably be some delegation down the ranks, especially in the larger companies where more ranks exist to delegate to. This is not simply a way of passing the buck. With all the aspects of CAD management, there are numerous clerical, technical, and managerial issues that need to be addressed. The CAD Manager may delegate many of these tasks, as the Project Manager will delegate many of theirs.

Whatever delegation takes place, the CAD system is still ultimately the responsibility of the CAD Manager, and the Project Manager is still ultimately responsible for the project.

Clear definitions of all individual and group responsibilities should be provided within a company's general QA Policy Manual. This will include the CAD Manager, whose duties may be described as:

> "responsible for monitoring the adequacy of the CAD system and making recommendations to the directors for its improvement."

Remember, however, that the responsibilities and job title of the CAD Manager tend to vary widely from company to company.

CAD Documentation

The preparation of the documents for a CAD department's QA policy involves knowing what documents are needed and how to go about creating them.

The documents

A successful quality system does the following:

- identifies everything that the company does
- presents this in written document form
- puts what has been written into practice
- is able to provide proof that it has been done

A QA system can be applied to any size of company. The company itself can write it, as long as every eventuality is covered adequately in the manual and each one is adhered to.

The biggest doubt about QA policy is that the amount of documentation will create a bureaucratic nightmare — so much that it actually hinders the work being done. This worry is unfounded; the whole intention of QA policy is to provide a structure of management processes that will improve efficiency and effectiveness. Any bureaucracy will therefore only be present as part of this process, so in fact all unnecessary paperwork and procedures will be discarded.

The auditors that accredit a company with the quality standard only require that staff do what it says in the manual. It is therefore important not to get carried away with documentation, setting unfeasible standards. For example, stating a compliance with an existing recognized standard may commit staff to an unnecessary and unattainable regime.

The person in charge of implementing the QA policy must be aware of the quantity and type of information that flows through the CAD department. Too often a person who is ignorant of computer technology will see a computer and presume it to simply be a big electronic calculator. Although this is actually true, it must be realized that in CAD applications a single computer may take on all the tasks previously done by a whole wine bar full of designers, visualizers, architects, etc., and must be subject to the same QA policy that they would have been.

Distinct from the main QA documentation that covers the Operating Procedures, documentation must exist to cover Drawing Techniques to indicate any standardization and other related items.

Documentation needs to be created to identify all processes, procedures, responsibilities, and resources that are implemented to achieve the company's objectives. Therefore, part of a company's QA Policy Manual will deal with the installation, maintenance, and operation of the computer systems (in our case, those that deal specifically with CAD).

After an initial investigation into the workings of a company, the QA consultant will come up with a list of documents, some involving more work than others. Here is a likely set of Operating Procedures documents relating to a CAD setup within a company:

- Register of approved computer programs
- Approval for purchase of new CAD software/hardware
- Record of calibration checks
- Computer maintenance record file
- Record of archived computer files
- Training records
- System documentation
- Standard Operating Procedures Manual (SOPM)
- Register of issues and updates of SOPM

Documented in the SOPM are instructions for CAD system and data management:

- Filing Systems
- Drawing Filenaming
- Backup Instructions
- Archive Instructions
- Disk Management
- Drawing History

- Drawing Versions
- Breakdown and Fault Recovery Systems
- Data Security
- Repair and Maintenance Arrangements
- Input Process
- Output Process

Involving the CAD staff

It is wise for the CAD Manager to involve the staff as much as possible in the preparation of the CAD QA documents. As well as the importance of not leaving staff in the dark about a course of action that will affect all employees, other good reasons exist for involving the CAD staff:

- They are the most qualified to comment on the working process. They do not have to follow a learning curve before being able to identify the important aspects of the working method to be documented.
- CAD departments are usually staffed by numerous individuals, each with their unique approach to the work. Each approach will contain valuable elements that will go toward an impressive policy.
- Staff that have participated in the creation of the system are more likely to accept it.
- It is necessary for accreditation that the QA process be evaluated continually and the documents subsequently modified. It is, therefore, important that staff are familiar enough with the policy to be able to do this. Taking part in the initial preparation gives them the appropriate experience and provides an understanding that is needed when alteration to working methods becomes necessary.
- It is quicker to delegate to CAD staff and cheaper than involving outsiders.

What to Do

- Use a QA Consultant in conjunction with a number of people — say, Project Managers, the CAD Manager, and the design team — to tackle the work involved in QA preparation.
- Clarify for each stage of the work process who shall be responsible for:
  - coordinating input
  - monitoring ongoing work
  - approving work at predetermined stages
  - deciding whether work will continue or change direction
  - coordinating output

- Together with the QA Consultant, come up with a list of documents to cover all Operating Procedures and a manual of Drawing Techniques. Identify all processes, procedures, responsibilities, and resources in preparation for creating documents.
- Involve staff as much as possible in their preparation.
- Put what has been written into practice.
- Be able to provide proof that it has been done.

The Operating Procedures documents:

- Register of approved computer programs
- Approval for purchase of new CAD software/hardware
- Record of calibration checks
- Computer maintenance record file
- Record of archived computer files
- Training records
- System documentation
- Standard Operating Procedures Manual (SOPM)
- Register of issues and updates of SOPM

Instructions for CAD data and system management:

- Filing Systems
- Drawing Filenaming
- Backup Instructions
- Archive Instructions
- Disk Management
- Drawing History
- Drawing Versions
- Breakdown and Fault Recovery Systems
- Data Security
- Repair and Maintenance Arrangements
- Input Process
- Output Process

Chapter

26

The Operating Procedures Documents

The CAD Operating Procedures documents form a part of the company's QA Policy manual and, as shown in the previous chapter, a likely set of documents would comprise the following:

- Register of approved computer programs
- Approval for purchase of new CAD software/hardware
- Record of calibration checks
- Computer maintenance record file
- Record of archived computer files
- Training records
- System documentation

Standard Operating Procedures Manual (SOPM):

- Filing Systems
- Drawing Filenaming
- Backup Instructions
- Archive Instructions
- Disk Management
- Drawing History
- Drawing Versions
- Breakdown and Fault Recovery Systems
- Data Security
- Repair and Maintenance Arrangements
- Input Process

- Output Process
- Register of issues and updates of SOPM

This chapter examines the contents of each individual document by providing information on the following:

Title: The title given to the document.

Function: The document's intended function.

Notes: A bulleted list of questions and considerations that must be taken into account. Most will be applicable to any CAD setup. Generally speaking, each document should (where appropriate) describe what is done when and by whom; and how it is checked, accepted, and recorded. There will also be details to note that relate specifically to an organization's particular operation.

Example: An example document from a fictitious company. It is not possible to create universal documentation that is applicable to all circumstances. If you wish you could use these examples as the basis for your own documentation and modify them to meet the specific requirements of your company.

Comment: A comment assessing how successful the given example is in achieving the intended function of the document.

Register of Approved Computer Programs

This document ensures that only suitable software is installed on each computer. Do and remember these things:

- All programs that are installed on the computers must be listed.
- Once created, there should be little need to amend it, apart from when new software is purchased.
- Name the people who are allowed to add to this list.
- Make this information clear and accessible to all users.

The example shown in Fig. 26-1 clearly indicates the software is available and on which CAD machine it can be used. For example, AutoCAD release 13 can only be used on the Sun computer. This may be because it is the only machine powerful enough to run release 13 at a suitable speed. Similarly, the word processing software (MS Word) is restricted to the PCs. This would prevent its being loaded onto other machines with different operating systems where it would not be suitable.

Approval for Purchase of New Computer Software/Hardware

This document prevents equipment being purchased without suitable justification. Do and remember these things:

"Register of approved computer programs"

The following software is approved for use by all CAD users on the computers specified.

Additions to this list can only be made by the CAD manager.

Approved software	From date	Computers
AEC (release 3.1)	12:03:89	all
PKZIP file compression utility	01:10:90	all
MSWord (version 7)	22:07:95	PCs only
AutoCAD (release 12)	12:02:93	all
AutoCAD (release 13)	09:01:95	SUN only

Figure 26-1. Example "Register of approved computer programs" document.

- Who can request the equipment and who can accept the request?
- Consider the intentions, expectations, and capabilities of the company.
- Give reasons for selecting all new, upgraded, in-house, and bought-in computer programs and hardware. These three tests are commonly used to assess possible purchases:
  - alternative comparison
  - independent verification
  - representative trials
- Publish results of the assessment.
- After the assessment, the document should be "signed off" maybe by the finance director — signifying acceptance of the purchase.
- Acceptance should assume adequate protection against software viruses.

In this example, we see the need being identified, the product choice being evaluated, and finally, the purchase being accepted. At each stage the CAD Manager is kept in check by other interested parties. This will prevent self-indulgence as well as the purchase of white elephants.

Record of Calibration Checks

This document provides information on equipment calibration. Do and remember these things:

- Specify equipment with reference numbers as well as a description.
- Name the person carrying out the check.
- Summarize the findings and the action to be taken.

"Approval for purchase of new CAD software/hardware"

Form completed by . . . .(CAD manager)   Date . . . .
Reason for purchase . . . .
Confirmation . . . . (Project manager)
Choice of alternatives . . . .
Method(s) used for evaluation . . . .
Results . . . .
Purchase authorization . . . . (Project manager)
Date . . . .
Acceptance of the purchase . . . . (Finance director)

Figure 26-2. Example "Approval for purchase of new CAD software/hardware" document.

"Record of calibration checks"

All calibration results are to be recorded here. If the findings necessitate further action, inform the CAD manager immediately.

Name of checker . . . .
Date . . . .
Equipment . . . .
Ref. no. . . . .
Findings . . . .
Outcome . . . .

Figure 26-3. Example "Record of calibration checks" document.

- Calibration and verification of the equipment used to calibrate and verify the CAD equipment should also be documented periodically.

Figure 26-3 shows a simple official record. The way that the routine maintenance is actually carried out is dealt with later in a part of the Standard Operating Procedures Manual. Once the CAD Manager has been informed about a discrepancy, a decision can be made whether or not to call the maintenance contractor, which would then be recorded in the following document.

Computer Maintenance Record File

This document provides details of equipment maintenance. Do and remember these things:

- Specify equipment with reference numbers as well as a description.
- Name the person carrying out maintenance.
- Summarize the findings and the action to be taken.

- Maintenance and verification of the equipment used to maintain and verify the CAD equipment should also be documented periodically.

"Computer maintenance record file"

All maintenance details to be recorded here.

Name . . . .   Date . . . .
Equipment . . . .
Ref. no. . . . .
Fault . . . .
Findings . . . .·. . . . .
Outcome . . . .

Figure 26-4. Example "Computer maintenance record file" document.

This is very similar to the calibration records. Again the procedures for such routine maintenance are dealt with later in the "Standard Operating Procedures Manual."

Record of Archived Computer Files

This document provides details of files and projects that have been archived. Do and remember these things:

- What is the file, when was it created, who worked on it, who archived it?
- The accuracy of the archived files must be verified.
- Up-to-date archive details would normally be held by the CAD Manager and the manager of the relevant project.
- The instructions for archiving are not mentioned here. They are found in the "Standard Operating Procedures Manual."

"Record of archived computer files"

Project name . . . .
Part of project archived . . . .
Number of archived copies . . . .
Where archive(s) are stored . . . .
List of files archived . . . .
Results of verification (by restoring sample files) . . . .
Name . . . .   (CAD manager) Date . . . .

Figure 26-5. Example "Record of archived computer files" document.

In the above example, note the "verification" line. This will act as a reminder to the archiver to check the success of the procedure. As this is only intended to be a record of files, sufficient information is contained here.

Training Records

This document provides information relating to staff training. Do and remember these things:

■ Training records would normally be documented by the CAD Manager.

■ The Personnel Manager should have a copy of this information in the personnel records.

■ Details from a periodic audit should exist to provide an up-to-date list of the CAD staff's skills.

■ The effectiveness of the training can be gauged from this information.

```
"Training records"

Copy to be given to personnel manager.

Name . . . . . . . . . . . . . . . . . . . . . . . . . . . . . . . . . . . . . . . . . . . . . . . . . . . . . . . . . .
Training received  . . . . . . . . . . . . . . . . . . . . . . . . . . . . . . . . . . . . . . . . . . . . . . . .
Name of trainer . . . . . . . . . . . . . . . . . . . . . . . . . . . . . . . . . . . . . . . . . . . . . . . . . .
Date(s)/times of course . . . . . . . . . . . . . . . . . . . . . . . . . . . . . . . . . . . . . . . . . .
Cost  . . . . . . . . . . . . . . . . . . . . . . . . . . . . . . . . . . . . . . . . . . . . . . . . . . . . . . . . . . . . .
Authorization . . . . . . . . . . . . . . . . . . . . . . . . . . . . . . . . . . . (CAD manager)
Summary of training to date  . . . . . . . . . . . . . . . . . . . . . . . . . . . . . . . . . . .
```

Figure 26-6. Example "Training record" document.

One of the simple forms shown in Fig. 26-6 would be completed each time a member of staff receives training. The actual training would follow the principles set out in the personnel training manual.

System Documentation

This document lists relevant details about the CAD system. Do and remember these things:

■ Note the make, model, and serial number of each individual element of the CAD hardware system, from mice to plotters.

■ Note the name, supplier, serial number, version, and revision of every copy of every software program included in the system.

- Describe the way memory is allocated on the hard disk.

- Explain the filing structure on the hard disk.

- The plotter setup (sometimes this may be stored on disk, or it may just be a matter of noting down plotter pen type and position) should be recorded.

- Include copies of digitizer overlays, especially if customized.

- Documentation should be of a sufficient standard for anyone to be able to refer to it when detailed system information is required—for instance, when requesting technical support over the telephone.

- It should be accessible to the whole CAD department but only created by a nominated person, usually the CAD Manager.

```
"System documentation"

Computer .....................   Brand .........................
Model .........................   Serial number ...................
CPU model ....................   CPU speed ......................
Math coprocessor model ..........   Hard disk size ..................
RAM .........................   Expanded/extended memory ........
Graphics board(s) brand ...........   Software details ................
CONFIG. SYS buffers ............   CONFIG. SYS files ..............
ACADFREERAM ................

Name ........................   (CAD manager)   Date ............
```

Figure 26-7. Example "System documentation" document.

This example indicates the amount of details that can be gone into for just a limited range of equipment. There is no point in me filling up pages with every detail of a fictitious company's CAD equipment. See the notes for more possibilities.

Standard Operating Procedures Manual (SOPM)

This document provides instruction for basic CAD usage. Each procedure is covered in subdocuments which are described next. Do and remember these things:

- It should be accessible for staff to refer to whenever they need to. Usually they are kept at hand by the CAD machines.

- It should be updated and redistributed regularly.

- The end of this chapter covers the register of issues and updates of SOPM.

Filing Systems

This document instructs on file storage and directory hierarchies. Do and remember these things:

- Who has the authority to create new directories/folders?
- When is it done? (preferably in one go at the start of a project)
- How are anomalies dealt with?
- The directory structure must be accessible and understandable. The situation must not arise where a CAD user cannot access a particular drawing.
- A record of the filing system procedure should be held (possibly in the Project folder).

"CAD Filing System"

    The CAD manager will create a directory on the CAD system with the project's name.
    A number of subdirectories will be created to hold the different elements of that project.
    Temporary drawings and Blocks should be stored in subdirectories of the main project directory named TEMP and BLOCKS.
    All directories are created on the network so as to make them accessible to all CAD machines.
    The "Dataman" file management program is used to create and modify directories.
    Any anomalies will be rectified during weekly system "housekeeping."

Example:
    A project to redesign gas station forecourts for "Power Petroleum" would contain a directory structure comprising a main directory called POWER with a subdirectory for each element of the project:

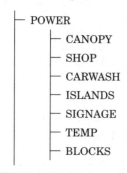

```
├─ POWER
│       ├─ CANOPY
│       ├─ SHOP
│       ├─ CARWASH
│       ├─ ISLANDS
│       ├─ SIGNAGE
│       ├─ TEMP
│       ├─ BLOCKS
```

Figure 26-8. Example "CAD Filing Systems" document.

■ Provision must be made for "unofficial" drawings, that is, temporary drawings or common elements (to be imported into the main drawings).

This example puts the onus on the CAD Manager to plan the best directory structure for a project. This is wise as it keeps a consistency throughout projects that would be lost if it were left to the individual users to interpret these instructions themselves.

Drawing Filenaming

This document explains the procedure for naming CAD files. Do and remember these things:

■ Names given to drawings would normally be decided on a project-wide basis rather than within the CAD department.

■ This naming policy must be accessible to anyone that may wish to view it (possibly held in the Project folder).

■ Be aware of the limitations of computer filenames such as the eight-character limit set by DOS.

■ The CAD Manager is usually responsible for the CAD filenaming procedure.

■ Temporary drawings and blocks should be clearly identified and there must be a procedure for dealing with anomalies.

"Drawing Filenaming"

Drawings are named according to the project's naming system (held in the project file) and CAD drawing filenames will correspond to this.
The maximum number of filename characters is eight.
Where common characters are used to denote the project name, these can be omitted in favor of an appropriately named subdirectory.
The name appearing in the drawings title blocks will be the full unabbreviated name.
Any temporary drawings and Blocks must be clearly identified, stored in their respective directories, and deleted when no longer required. During the weekly machine "housekeeping," any anomalies will be rectified.
Similar drawings may be stored in a single CAD drawing file. See the "Drawing Versions" document for details.

Example:
POSTDD16 is a typical drawing name from the "Power" project. The first two characters (PO) are the same for all drawings in this project and simply refer to Power. A CAD drawing with this name would, therefore, omit the first two characters to be called STDD16 and be stored in the POWER directory.

Figure 26-9. Example "Drawing Filenaming" document.

■ Any shortcuts or simplification of filenames should be apparent.

It is clear in the example shown in Fig. 26-9 that filenaming is a project responsibility rather than a purely CAD responsibility. As well as advising on the naming policy, the CAD Manager would deal with the practicalities of implementing it in his department.

Backup Instructions

This document provides a procedure for the duplication of ongoing work as precaution against loss or damage to the working file. Do and remember these things:

■ Backup procedures need to be regimented and regularly monitored.

■ There must be no gaps in what is backed up.

■ Daily, weekly, monthly, full, incremental—a procedure must be given for each type of backup.

■ Consider the time taken to perform a backup; in larger CAD setups sufficient time should be allocated, as it could take quite a while.

■ If a procedure involves customized programs, they should be detailed.

■ The frequency of backup and any additional notes that are required to accompany backups should be specified.

■ Procedures must be documented for each type of backup media available.

■ How is backup media stored before and after backing up?

■ Are additional copies required?

■ At what point can old backup media be overwritten?

■ How is the backed up information to be stored?

Figure 26-10 shows that two types of media are available for backing up in this company. They are covered in sufficient detail for CAD operators to be able to follow the procedures without further assistance. Additional information, such as the CAD Manager performing full system backups every 6 months, provides the operator with useful background knowledge as well as clarifying the CAD Manager's instructions.

Archive Instructions

This document gives instructions regarding the long-term storage of completed work. Do and remember these things:

"Backup Instructions"

Floppy disks:
- For "personal" backing up.
- CAD users are responsible for backing up their own work and cataloging it in accordance with project instructions.
- Disks and disk holders available from disk store cupboard.
- Backing up should be performed at least at the end of each day, unless instructed to do otherwise by the project manager or CAD manager.
- Disks should be stored in the designated project disk holder unless the project file contains instructions for them to be stored elsewhere.
- Disks are to be clearly labeled with details of operator, project, and department.
- The original files should be left on the computer only to be removed by the CAD manager.

Tape:
- For "emergency" backing up and restoration only.
- Blank tapes are held in the "tape cabinet" by the CAD manager's desk.
- Full-drawing backups to tape will be performed on the first weekday of each month by the CAD manager before work commences (or by the senior CAD operator if the CAD manager is not available).
- Incremental-drawing backups to tape will be performed on each Friday, at the end of work, by the CAD manager (or by the senior CAD operator if the CAD manager is away).
- Full-system backups to tape will be performed six per month or, if significant changes have been made to systems files, at appropriate times, by the CAD manager (or by the senior CAD operator if the CAD manager is away).
- After each backup is made, the date will be written on the tape label along with other relevant information such as the number in the sequence, etc.
- Only automated tape backup commands will be used — as understood by the CAD manager. Restoration of information from tape may only be performed by the CAD manager.
- Tapes will be removed after backing up and stored off-site.
- All tape backups are recorded in a register, held with the tapes.

Figure 26-10. Example "Backup Instructions" document.

- When is it to be performed?
- How is it to be performed?
- Who is authorized to carry it out?
- Must satisfy legal requirements.
- What defines work as suitable for archiving?
- A verification procedure should be implemented, to identify "faulty" media, for instance.
- What happens to the original work after archiving?

- Under what conditions are archives stored?
- Is more than one archive to be made? Sometimes a duplicate will be held off-site in a safe, for example.
- The restoring procedure.
- If someone wishes to restore archived work, how do they go about it? For instance, a request could be made to the CAD Manager who will then deal with the request accordingly.
- Procedures to archive and then restore must be workable and possible for many years to come.

"Archive Instructions"

A project's CAD component will be archived by the CAD manager when the project is completed (as indicated by the project manager).

This will involve the complete removal of the project data from the hard disk.

One archive will be stored in the off-site safe.

Copies will be made if requested (for the project file, for example).

All archives are made using tapes from the tape cabinet next to the CAD manager's desk. They must be labeled with date, project details, and any other information considered relevant.

Verification: Once every 2 months a tape approximately 6 months old and a recent tape archive are to be restored and the data checked for completeness.

Figure 26-11. Example "Archive Instructions" document.

Not a great deal of detail is presented in this example document, but it says that it is the CAD Manager's responsibility to archive completed projects, and presuming they are trained to do so, there is no need to discuss the mechanics of the procedure in detail.

Disk Management

This document is used to ensure that the computer remains free of unwanted files. Do and remember these things:

- Files that are "dead" and any anomalies must be dealt with by a designated person, usually the CAD Manager.
- What is meant by "dealt with" should be clarified.
- Similarly backup media should be checked for any anomalies or incompleteness and rectified accordingly.
- A certain amount of temporary and junk files are acceptable but only within the confines of the time and frequency of the disk "housekeeping," which must be specified.

"Disk Management"

The CAD manager is the only person authorized to perform disk "housekeeping" — that is, the removal of unwanted files and the correction of any anomalies in file and directory naming and structure.
This takes place on the last working day of each week and applies to the hard disk and any short-term backup media.
Any rogue files will be held only for as long as they can be identified and then kept or erased.

Figure 26-12. Example "Disk Management" document.

This example warns any sloppy user that disk housekeeping takes place, routinely encouraging them to abide by the other file management procedures.

Drawing History

This document records all relevant drawing details. Do and remember these things:

- Sufficient information of drawing history must be available, possibly held on a drawing title block.
- Even quick sketches must be identified.
- This would normally involve the person who checks completed work.
- Standard ink stamps could be used to designate the state of a drawing ("passed" or "rework necessary," for example).

This documentation would be enhanced if a standard title block were held on the computer. This would then act as a prompt for the information required.

"Drawing History"

Each drawing must contain a standard title block.
As well as the drawing name, the title block should include details of revisions, the date that they were made, and if appropriate, who the drawing is for (project designer, client, etc.).
Rough sketches must contain sufficient information to relate them to the project.
Any drawing not containing appropriate information runs the risk of becoming detached from the rest of the project and removed during the weekly disk housekeeping.

Figure 26-13. Example "Drawing History" document.

Drawing Versions

This document allows identification of a particular drawing among similar versions, possibly created within a single drawing file. Do and remember these things:

- A way of clarifying this potentially confusing situation must be described clearly.

- This procedure, like many others in this chapter, deals with a problem also encountered by manual drafters. Therefore, such procedures are likely to exist already.

"Drawing Versions"

Where more than one version of the same drawing are to be worked on, follow one of these two procedures:
1. Allocate separate drawing filenames according to the project naming system.
2. Keep all versions in a single CAD file. The filename should be a generic name and the layer names reflect the version that they hold.

Example:
A series of similar drawings could either be called:
TLCOT01, TLCOT02, TLCOT03
They could also all be stored in one drawing called TLCOT, with each version held on layers 01, 02, and 03, respectively.

Figure 26-14. Example "Drawing Versions" document.

This example document, as well as offering a procedure for dealing with the problem of drawing versions, indicates that it can be avoided by adhering properly to the project's naming system.

Breakdown and Fault Recovery Systems

This document instructs on responding to any kind of software and hardware disruption. Do and remember these things:

- Include hardware, system files, and work files in the procedure.
- Who is authorized to follow this procedure?
- Take into account the scale of the breakdown. There is no point restoring the whole system when only one accidentally deleted file is involved.
- Include details of any organized service agreement and where the information is held.

> "Breakdown and Fault Recovery Systems"
>
> CAD users must report any error messages, potential hazards, and so on, as soon as is possible to the CAD manager. This includes everything from a mysterious file to an unusually high/low room temperature.
>
> If necessary, all or part of the drawing and system database can be recovered from the tapes (which are stored off-site). Alternatively, there is the option of restoring from the floppy disks when requiring only a small number of files.
>
> This process must only take place when the original work is definitely lost, and only by the CAD manager. The senior CAD designer will do this, should the CAD manager not be available.
>
> When a hardware breakdown occurs, the CAD manager will have the first attempt at resolving the situation. Should this not be sufficient, the CAD manager will contact the company that we hold a maintenance agreement with (Cadfix Ltd.)
>
> This agreement includes guaranteed response times and the replacement of defunct equipment. Details of the agreement and procedure are available at the CAD manager's desk should he not be available.
>
> Project managers will be kept informed of the loss of any equipment.
>
> Details of faults will be recorded by the CAD manager in the "Computer Maintenance Record File."

Figure 26-15. Example "Breakdown and Fault Recovery Systems" document.

The mention of the maintenance agreement in the example allows the document to be greatly simplified. Basically, what is being said is that the CAD Manager will deal with all faults by calling the maintenance support company if necessary.

Data Security

This document details security measures that are relevant to the CAD system. Do and remember these things:

- When new staff are employed ensure that all equipment can be operated properly and procedures followed.

- Companywide problems (such as theft, fire, flood, and power surges) are irrelevant here.

- The reliance that design companies place on freelancers poses a security problem that must be addressed.

- Office procedures and passwords and so on are worthwhile considering.

- A suitable password is as long as possible (usually 8 characters), involving alphabetic and numeric characters, an unusual word, not so personal that it may be guessed, regularly altered, not written down or told to unauthorized people.

- Users with knowledge of any password systems being used should be noted in a register of authorized users.

- Similar restrictions should be placed on users of any add-on programs and customized routines.

- Anti-virus procedures are also covered under this heading.

Figure 26-16 shows a departmental security policy that will be combined with a companywide one. The essence of this procedure is a combination of preventative measures and "tell the CAD Manager of anything suspicious."

"Data Security"

All data security violations must be reported to the CAD manager along with any evidence.

New passwords are implemented on the first working day of each month by the CAD manager and distributed personally to all CAD staff. It is then the responsibility of the CAD staff to ensure security is not breached. No passwords should be kept written down or on computer. Any loss of password information should be reported to the CAD manager who will then issue new passwords.

Those issued with the password will have their names recorded.

Certain areas of the computer system will have a password to restrict access to the CAD manager only.

All tape backup and archive material will be stored off-site as soon as is possible after use.

The CAD manager will check for viruses during the Disk Management procedure.

It is the responsibility of all CAD operators to use the Virus Scanning software installed on the CAD machines whenever a floppy disk is being issued or received. If a virus should be found, it must be reported to the CAD manager immediately.

Figure 26-16. Example "Data Security" document.

Repair and Maintenance Arrangements

This document provides procedures for maintaining all CAD equipment. Do and remember these things:

- Maintenance contract details should be readily accessible.

- The choice of companies providing this support should be justified in a way similar to that used when purchasing software and hardware.

- All CAD repair and maintenance is usually instigated and monitored by the CAD Manager.

- The routine maintenance tasks that are regularly repeated, such as pen cleaning, should be described.

- You may only wish to calibrate/maintain only when you have reason to believe there is a need. If so, that is fine, as long as the procedure is documented and you stick to it.

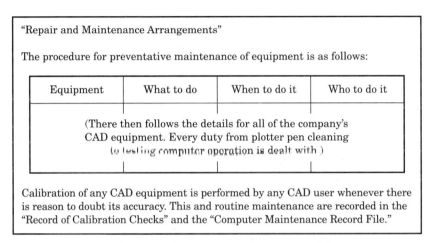

"Repair and Maintenance Arrangements"

The procedure for preventative maintenance of equipment is as follows:

Equipment	What to do	When to do it	Who to do it

(There then follows the details for all of the company's CAD equipment. Every duty from plotter pen cleaning to testing computer operation is dealt with.)

Calibration of any CAD equipment is performed by any CAD user whenever there is reason to doubt its accuracy. This and routine maintenance are recorded in the "Record of Calibration Checks" and the "Computer Maintenance Record File."

Figure 26-17. Example "Repair and Maintenance Arrangements" document.

The calibration/maintenance policy indicated in Fig. 26-17 is relatively casual. Some companies may wish to maintain and calibrate everything at regular intervals. This casual approach is fine, as long as you say what you do, then do what you say.

Input Process

This document advises on assessing initial data. Do and remember these things:

- Whenever a DXF (or similar) transfer of data has taken place, procedures for verifying completeness of transfer must be followed.

- This may involve a "work checker" to check correctness by (for instance) referring to a hardcopy.

- Confusion can occur when discrepancies appear between symbols, datum points, accuracy, and so on, with different sources of survey information.

- Scanning is still a developing technology and so offers a wide variety of methods and qualities of output. Does the output reach an acceptable standard?

- Imported CAD data must conform to standards set for in-house CAD work for, say, layering conventions and dimension styles.
- It must be made clear who is responsible for all this information.
- Consider a disclaimer, possibly incorporated in the title block.

"Input Process"

It is the responsibility of the CAD designer to verify the quality of their source data whatever form it is in. Any problems must be reported to the CAD manager and the relevant project manager.

Figure 26-18. Example "Input Process" document.

The example shown in Fig. 26-18 may look like a cop-out on what could be a very lengthy and detailed document. Although this fictitious company has avoided that, the procedure has still been specified, no matter how generalized it is. No rule exists that says all procedures must be lengthy and complex.

Output Process

This document advises on assessing output data. Do and remember these things:

- Take into account the many possible selections that can be taken from the total drawing information. The selection is made using methods such as PLOT Window, LAYER Freeze, and Thaw, etc.
- The state of the layers at the time of plotting should be mentioned as well as plotter settings and pen thickness/color.
- A distinction between "final" plots and "intermediate" plots should be made.
- When a drawing is issued, the project management procedures should be followed.
- Sufficient information must accompany data when output takes the form of disks, modem transmissions, and so on, such as fonts, print-outs, and listings.
- At what point does responsibility for the work lie/cease to lie with the CAD Operator/CAD Manager?
- Ensure that unrequired plots and so on are discarded.

In this example, once again, all the consideration points have been dealt with by a single, generalized statement. That is, when the work is in the hands of the CAD designer, the output is their responsibility.

"Output Process"

It is the responsibility of th CAD designer to check the quality of their output data, whatever form it is in. Any problems must be reported to the CAD manager and the relevant project manager.

Figure 26-19. Example "Output Process" document.

This does not act as a guarantee of high quality. It depends on the quality levels of the CAD designers. If a company is unable to spend the time and effort scrutinizing every output, then their Output Process document should say so, as this one does.

Register of Issues and Updates of Standard Operating Procedures Manual

This document records the names of people who have been issued with a copy of the latest SOPM. Note:

- It is wise to keep track of the copies of such an important manual.
- You must know for sure who has a copy of the latest version to counter any pleas of ignorance from staff caught not following the procedures.

The procedures held in the Standard Operating Procedures Manual will be available to all CAD users. The example below will record who has got it and when.

"Register of Issues and Updates of Standard Operating Procedures Manual"

Date of most recent update ....
Names of those issued with the Manual and date of issue
....
....
Signed .... (CAD manager)   Date ....

Figure 26-20. Example "Register of Issues and Updates of Standard Operating Procedures Manual" document.

What to Do

Ensure that each Operating Procedures document, where possible, describes:

What is done.

When it is done.

Who does it.

How it is checked.

How it is accepted.

How it is recorded.

27

The Drawing Procedures Manual

Every CAD department should possess a manual that comprises the "house rules" for drawings. A collection of instructions covering settings, standards, and style will provide the guidelines for the designer to work within.

In this chapter I offer a checklist of generic points to be considered when compiling CAD drawing procedures. The work an organization is involved in will partly dictate the drawing standards that are laid down. Something that is crucial in one sector may be considered trivial in another.

If a company has existing standards for manual drafting it is not too difficult to adapt them to apply to CAD techniques. There is a danger of getting carried away and creating an excessively long list of drawing standards that would be unworkable in practice. It is essential, therefore, to target all the essential points, but leave the designer sufficient freedom to work within these rules.

A large proportion of the points mentioned can be incorporated in a prototype drawing as discussed in Chapter 20. This would greatly simplify the task of implementing drawing procedures. The prototype drawing can be combined with a Drawing Procedures Manual which would cover any remaining procedures that are still left to the designer.

In this chapter I am purely concerned with examining the documentation of drawing procedures as if forming part of a company's Quality Assurance system. A broader discussion on the subject of drawing style and standards can be found in Chapter 20.

Features of a Drawing Procedures Manual

There follows some common features of a Drawing Procedures Manual along with a look at concerns relating to each one. Where I refer to

CAD commands I use the command names from the AutoCAD software package. Similar and comparable names and functions exist in most other CAD packages.

Menus Identical command menus must be available to every CAD operator, and be held along with the drawing file after work has finished so it is automatically there when the file is opened in the future.

Layers Define the name, status (thawed/frozen, on/off), color, and linetype of each layer according to the requirements of the project.

It is easy to create additional layers during CAD work, but this is unacceptable when more than one user is involved and particularly when the CAD file is to be sent to a client as problems arise if a drawing containing unauthorized layers is used with other programs to create a bill of materials, for instance.

So, decide on a layering convention and stick to it throughout the project so that it is a framework accepted as the way of working by the staff.

Blocks (grouped drawing elements) Are they created on layer 0 or on the target layer? Are standard insertion points to be used? Once blocks are inserted, are operators allowed to "explode" them? This could disrupt programs that analyze the Block content of the drawing.

With title blocks, for example, rules may be laid down regarding when they can be inserted, before commencing the drawing or on completion.

Entities They can all keep their default settings of color, linetype, layer, and so on, or be modified to possess new customized properties.

Text styles Define the styles that are permissible and provide instructions on when and where they are to be used. Specify name, font, height, width factor, and so on.

Units Conform to the same form of units throughout the project and indicate this in the title box.

Views Standard on-screen views can be defined. This also serves to provide standardized layouts for plotted output.

Dimensions The dimension style is open to personal interpretation. The numerous Dimensioning Variables can be set to define all elements of the style and position of dimensions. For example, the size and type of the arrowhead used is something that may be considered that will make a dramatic effect to the appearance of a piece of work (see Fig. 27-1).

System variables Fix the value of these variables. Some are simple on/off toggles, while others are more versatile. For a description of system variables and what they can do, see Chapter 20.

Industry standards Relevant aspects of recognized drawing standards may be followed (BS 1192, for example).

Origin Usually this would be at coordinates 0,0,0, but it can be altered. People tend to presume the origin to be there and will get upset when they insert one of your drawings into one of theirs and find

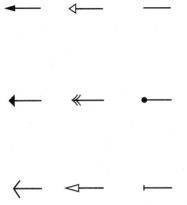

Figure 27-1. Define a dimension arrowhead.

it is incorrectly positioned. Therefore, QA standards should fix and guarantee 0,0,0 as the origin.

Saving work This must be done every X minutes by the operator or enforced with the aid of an automated saving program.

Ending "Zoom to extents, set to layer zero, . . ." The way that a drawing is ended defines the environment that will be present when recommencing work at a later date.

Revisions It is difficult to keep track of revisions. Add-on programs can be used to automatically prompt the user for revision details before a plot is done. Instructions regarding how and when a revision is created should exist.

Checking The time for checking a drawing must be identified as must the person performing the checking. A method for confirming that the drawing complies with the standards laid out here needs to be instituted. Therefore, work should be checked on computer to allow the verification of layer compliance and so on, rather than just assessing the visual appearance of the drawing.

What to Do

- Create a Drawing Procedures Manual as a guide to the company's CAD drawing style.

- Derive CAD drawing procedures partly from existing traditional methods and partly from new CAD-specific elements such as menus, layers, blocks, entities, text styles, units, views, dimensions, and so on.

9

Financial Management

The whole thrust behind this book is that CAD is not an electronic drawing board but a complete design tool with companywide repercussions, and that it should be managed accordingly.

It is appropriate, therefore, that the final part of this book is dedicated to the issue that has the final word in all other business decisions: money.

Unless a company's CAD facility is financially justifiable, its tremendous potential will go unexploited and it will become nothing more than a token gesture toward technology. It is vital, therefore, to identify and manage the true costs and returns of the CAD investment.

Financial analysis is made difficult by the fact that many benefits of the technology are not apparent until later on in the design-to-manufacture process. This part of the book explains how these benefits can be traced and quantified. The concepts of costing and charging are investigated, as is their ultimate objective — the CAD Cost Center, a financially independent business within a business.

Chapter

28

Investment and Returns

The precise methods of financial accounting do not work very well when dealing with intangible factors. This is often the case with CAD, where its costs are only too well known but the returns often border on the anecdotal. Even when it is clear that more projects are being completed to a higher standard, or that the manufacturers are getting it right the first time instead of on repeated attempts, it is difficult to tie it objectively to CAD techniques and quantify it financially.

This chapter looks at the initial expense of CAD and then the prospect of financial returns on the investment.

Investment

Anyone purchasing computer equipment soon learns that, although short-term costs can be reduced by buying cheap, the longer term may prove more expensive than had the higher price been paid initially. This is because no savings occur if further amounts of time and money are needed to make the equipment perform as desired — apparent for anything from just buying memory for a computer to networking a whole system.

This doesn't mean that the more money spent, the better, just that you shouldn't cut corners to save a few pennies in the short run, as it will probably cost you dollars in the long run. In the CAD world, it makes sense to buy too much rather than too little. Imagine a busy CAD department, with the workload rising to the bursting point and the pressure of the deadline looming over the staff. If "too much" has been bought, then the CAD system will behave as predicted, no problem; if "too little" has been bought, then problems will arise, with no way to fix them. The work will progress as well as a car touring the Alps with an engine too puny to take it over the Pennines.

You must ensure that new equipment will do exactly what it is intended to do before the purchase is made. The salesperson will say that it meets all the requirements, but you must be sure. Once the equipment has been proved appropriate beyond doubt, then negotiate the best deal that you can.

The sticking point here is getting the Finance Director (or whomever authorizes large-scale purchases in the company) to part with the money. To this person, the best deal is necessarily the cheapest, and it's often difficult to explain why this might not be the case. Also, discussing the specifics of a particular work example will be pointless if she does not possess any CAD knowledge. Here is a useful quote that explains the principle well:

> It's unwise to pay too much, but it's worse to pay too little. When you pay too much, you lose a little money—and that's all. When you pay too little, you sometimes lose everything, because the thing you bought was incapable of doing the thing it was bought to do. The common law of business balance prohibits paying a little and getting a lot, but it can't be done. If you deal with the lowest bidder, it is well to add something for the risk you run, and if you do that you will have enough to pay for something better.   —JOHN RUSKIN (1819–1900)

Returns

How can the word "payback" be applied to a "way of working" such as CAD? It is like trying to account for a business system like Quality Assurance or Concurrent Engineering. Is there an appropriate accounting system to deal with this sort of thing?

The payback

When calculating the profitability of the CAD investment, a number of figures must be considered:

- hardware costs
- software costs
- total overheads per hour
- CAD man-hours
- length of CAD learning curve
- productivity (before, during, and after learning curve)

These kind of figures can yield information on the costs and the revenue resulting from CAD's introduction. The last one —productivity— is a contentious issue. Despite the fact that CAD is a completely different approach to design from the drawing board method, salespeople will compare the two directly and say that CAD is 3, 4, or 5 times more productive than manual design techniques. This comment is misleading. This doesn't mean that CAD will not increase productivity, but that it's just inappropriate to use the sort of clear-cut figures more suited to evaluating the performance increase due to replacing a widget machine with a bigger widget machine. With design work, other considerations must be taken into account, such as the type of work being done and whether extra work actually exists to allow productivity to increase.

Analysis of these figures does not come under the job description of the CAD Manager but is a task for an experienced accountant. However, the CAD Manager should have these figures at hand, not least because they can yield the payback period—the time period needed to allow the original investment to be returned.

Two types of payback are apparent after the introduction of CAD into the workplace:

- on-off cost savings

- ongoing and wide-ranging revenue raising repercussions

The first is a single reduction of costs or increased revenue. This may arise, for example, from less reliance on freelancers and outside contractors to perform tasks that can be accomplished using CAD.

The second type of payback reduces day-to-day costs and/or increases day-to-day income due to the effects of CAD that are felt "further down the line" (such as shorter lead times, for instance).

The need for appropriate accounting systems

There are a number of potential problems when accounting for CAD. In today's computerized world most accounting personnel will be familiar with technology used to process figures. However, the use of technology to process graphical images may be an alien concept to them. This lack of understanding must be addressed, otherwise the CAD investment will be mishandled by the accounts department.

By far the most common failing of those accounting for CAD is the apparent oversight in tracking down the financial rewards that are a result of its wide-ranging influence. This miscalculation is represented in Fig. 28-1. If these "phantom" financial returns are not identified, CAD is not being credited with the success that it is responsible for and benefits may instead be attributed to other areas of the enterprise.

As well as reflecting badly on the whole CAD department, this ignorance of CAD's repercussions will distort any analysis of the company's finances. Yet, alarmingly, most people are blissfully unaware when this oversight occurs.

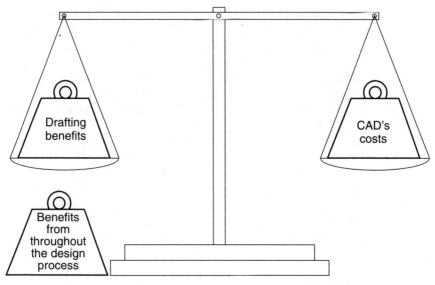

Figure 28-1. All financial returns must be identified to outweigh CAD's costs.

A company's accounting method must address the special nature of the CAD investment and not overlook ongoing paybacks. The financial rewards it brings, especially over the long run, are complex and widespread.

The numerous advantages of CAD, as discussed in Chapter 3, not only benefit the design process, but they can enhance the work of those not directly involved in design. For example, increased success in pitching for new work may be credited to those doing the pitching when in fact it is due to the improved quality and information content of the (CAD) drawings that are being presented.

The more a design business is analyzed, the more benefits will be discovered that arise as an indirect result of CAD techniques. Here are some examples:

- improvements in design quality
- reductions in scrap
- speeding up of the design-to-manufacture process
- improved staff motivation

It is not easy to put a figure on these benefits, but others are even more subjective. For instance, can you put a value on the increase in sales resulting from the simple fact that a client knows you have CAD? Or a job completed earlier than otherwise, allowing you to take on a new, high-earning job?

To attribute such rewards to the CAD department, they must be identified and then altered from seemingly intangible and vague to tangible and objective figures.

For example, training is a specific area of CAD expenditure where it is difficult to quantify the financial rewards. How can it be financially justified? Training is the key to unlocking the potential from a CAD system that has cost a lot of money. It is usually subjectively inspired, but link training to business objectives and it can be evaluated in a more objective way. So, training in 3-D visualization, for instance, will relieve the company of the cost of employing an artist. Similarly the cost of failing to take advantage of training should be considered, that is, the expense of underutilized equipment, poor work, and staff absenteeism. This businesslike justification of training is discussed extensively in Chapter 13.

Accounting for CAD requires that all costs and returns are considered over time. Calculating the complete payback as, say, yearly figures, gives accountants something tangible to work with. Savings resulting from long-term and indirect benefits can then be identified. Hopefully this will be sufficient to meet initial costs and provide a profit that will more than compensate for the risk and disruption caused by the introduction of CAD.

The figures used do not need to be precise. For instance, a single amount may be estimated to cover "reduced manufacturing costs" that would include every benefit related to manufacturing from reduced reworking to providing CAD data that is compatible with manufacturing technology.

What to Do

- Where CAD is concerned, do not cut corners to save a few pennies in the short run as it will cost dollars in the long run.

- Ensure that new equipment does exactly what is required of it before the investment is made.

- Be aware of the two types of payback resulting from the CAD investment; on-off cost savings and the ongoing and wide ranging revenue raising repercussions.

- Attribute all intangible benefits to the CAD department by relating them to business objectives and the time over which they accrue.

Chapter

29

Cost Management

Whatever method of accounting a company operates, it's wise to monitor the finances of the CAD department closely. As more and more work involves CAD techniques, so the amount of money spent on the resource must rise. It makes sense to charge some costs to individual clients and for others to be spread across the whole company. Charging a client for the CAD facility requires the identification of actual costs and the time over which those costs are to be recovered.

Costing and charging are two separate but related activities that together comprise cost management. Figure 29-1 outlines the basic idea behind each one.

This chapter examines each activity by first listing the benefits it brings about and then discussing the process of specifying figures.

	Costing	Charging
Planning	Establish a unit of cost for each CAD activity	Establish a price list of charges for each item
Implementation	Monitor actual costs and compare with the planned cost unit	Compile and issue invoices

Figure 29-1. Costing and charging for CAD services.

Monitoring Costs

CAD is a far-reaching activity with far-reaching costs. The range of benefits that are gained from monitoring these costs are equally far-reaching.

The benefits of costing

- Decisions about services can be made on cost effectiveness, that is, the quality of service and expenditure can be balanced.
- Investment can be planned in a businesslike way.
- Expenditure can be justified.
- Planning and budgeting can be tackled with confidence.
- New or better business opportunities can be identified.
- There is an incentive to improve the quality, speed, and value of the service.

Specifying costs

The figures used when discussing CAD finance seem high to those whose experience of drawing office expenditure is a box of pencils. As well as the initial costs, there are ongoing costs to consider. However, the benefits that CAD can bring are undoubtedly enormous (see Chapter 3). If the right approach is taken the costs can be managed and the business can reap the rewards. Put simply, the costs of providing the service must be known; otherwise, there's no prospect of maximizing value for money.

It is important to include the cost of training, development, and so on, because things that lead to improved efficiency can in turn reduce income. For example, we know that revising a drawing is vastly simpler with CAD than manual techniques. If only the cost of making the revision were considered, the charge would be minimal. The true cost is calculated by including an additional element relating to the costs of training and CAD investment to the final bill.

Let us look at the full range of costs.

Outgoings

1. Systems and software:
   - Hardware
     computers + peripherals
     plotters
     extras, cabling, etc.
   - Hardware upgrades (memory, processors, etc.)
   - In-house software development
   - Bought-in (new) software ·
   - Software upgrades/licenses
2. Maintenance and consumables:
   - Maintenance contracts
   - Maintenance (noncontract)

- Disks
- Tapes
- Paper
- Pens/ink/toner
3. Staff:
    - Salaries
    - Expenses
    - Office services
    - Training
    - Books
4. Support:
    - Troubleshooting
    - Disaster prevention/recovery

This list could be extended further to include such things as transportation and accommodation.

Depreciation Depreciation measures the reduction in the value of something over its useful life. Therefore, it must be considered when preparing a list of costs. A charge for depreciation is made so that a fair proportion of the total cost is allocated to each accounting period. So, to calculate the depreciation value of something's initial cost or value, its useful life and its value at the end of this period must be known.

A figure for depreciation of an item can be arrived at by:

- Dividing the total cost into equal segments for each period.
- Taking a fixed percentage of the remaining value each period.
- Taking a value proportional to the usage in each period.

Recovery time The time period over which costs are to be recovered ("chargeable machine time") needs to be known. It is inaccurate to say that a CAD designer is productive for 48 weeks times 40 hours per year. Calculations must include sufficient time for:

- Preparation and software development before the project starts.
- Staff training.
- Cleaning, maintenance, etc.
- Workload procedures preparation
- Software tools could be used to collate this sort of data.

Work time It is not as straightforward to predict the time that will be spent on a particular job as it would seem at first. Numerous factors can influence the time taken for the same worker to complete the same piece of work:

- The experience of the CAD designer.
- Whether the staff are already familiar with the project.
- Staff motivation.
- The standard and reliability of the hardware/software.
- The working environment.
- The level of system support.

Bear in mind that the CAD usage often increases toward the end of a project (think of the time spent on preliminary drawings compared with final detailed drawings).

A point at which the work is finished must be defined. This is especially important with more "intelligent" CAD drawings that become inextricably linked with other parts of the design process. (This "intelligence" is, after all, one of the reasons you will be using CAD.) This may result in regular reentry into the "completed" drawing, increasing the work time.

As long as these warnings are noted, it should be possible to come up with a figure for the time taken to complete the work.

Setting Charges

A consequence of monitoring costs is the question, "Where does the money come from to pay for them?" Income is generated in two ways. First, by completing projects and being paid by the client, and second, by charging for CAD usage. It is this second approach that I describe here.

The benefits of charging

- Customers and CAD designers become aware of the costs of the services provided and view CAD as a commodity not to be wasted.
- The customer can expect a specific service for a specific price. If they think the service is not value for money they can use alternatives or complain to the management.
- Cost-recovery considerations can be used to justify CAD expenditure.
- CAD costs can be recovered in a fair manner, related to usage.
- Customer behavior can be influenced, for example, by offering lower prices for off-peak usage.

Specifying charges

Although CAD may be viewed as an important utility within the company it is all too often treated as a free utility. In addition, the increasing role played by CAD coupled with its complex nature, has resulted in rising budgets without the actual running costs being identified.

When setting a charge for CAD usage, consider the costs that are incurred (as described previously in this chapter) and what it is that the customer (whether inside or outside the company) is actually getting for their money. (For example, besides just a series of CAD drawings on a disk, the client also receives long-term benefits as described in Chapter 28.)

The CAD Cost Center

The term used to describe a department placed under a strictly cost-managed regime is a Cost Center.

Any CAD department should consider becoming an independent Cost Center within the parent company — a part of the overall business in which both expenditure and revenue are controlled independently. The result is that the performance of that particular business segment can be evaluated.

Not all situations will obviously lend themselves to this kind of regime. A small company in which everyone uses their personal CAD terminal on their desk may not be able to ring-fence the effects of CAD from any other part of their work. The issues discussed, however, are still very applicable and important for cost control, maximizing the utilization of resources, and for making businesslike evaluations of the CAD facility.

Whether your department already is a Cost Center, you are considering making it such, or you have no idea about how (in)efficient you currently are, the principles and methods involved in a Cost Center are good ones and still worth following. They will give a clear understanding of costs and how they are identified relating to the various activities of the CAD department. Then charges can be set appropriately for each "unit" of business, allowing the costs to be recovered.

Planning and implementation

First of all, the following matters need to be clarified:

- Do you want the CAD department to aim for profits or just to cover costs?
- What are the likely benefits of cost management?
- What resources and costs are incurred by cost management?

- Do prospective customers have meaningful budgets with which they can plan their expenditure?
- To what degree are invoices and so on integrated into existing accounting systems?
- Who pays the bills in each of the various possible situations?
- What is, and is not, to be included as "costs" (i.e., furniture, training)?
- What are the rules for charging when disciplines become blurred?

Then, charges need to be calculated. A procedure for doing this is shown in Fig. 29-2. Here costs and workload are estimated over a fixed period. Income is constantly monitored and charges recalculated accordingly.

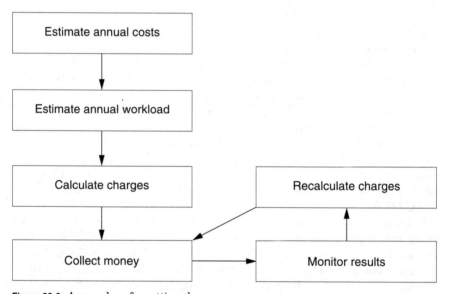

Figure 29-2. A procedure for setting charges.

There are numerous ways of calculating prices. A simple example is shown here:

If Total annual costs = C and Chargeable machine hours = T,
then Charge = C/T dollars per hour

This would give a single charge based on the amount of CAD time used, regardless of what was actually being done. Customers could be charged per hour or by agreeing to a fixed rate before the work starts.

An alternative method is to calculate a different charge for every service, so that the final price is arrived at by adding up each element:

Development + basic 2-D work + 3-D modeling + A1 pen plots + A0 electrostatic plots + pens/ink + cataloging + disks + . . .

Once a satisfactory method of charging has been decided upon, remember these things:

- Document all procedures (weekly, monthly, yearly) and provide training when implementing the Cost Center as it involves procedures that may be totally unfamiliar to those involved.

- As much, if not all, the accounting work should be done by the company's accounts department rather than the CAD department.

- Use worksheets (either manual or computer based) to gather usage data.

- Project managers must be made aware of new processes and working methods

Ongoing appraisal

Reviews of the cost management system should take place over specific periods.

Daily/Weekly

- Ongoing collection of cost and charging data.

- Instigate changes if necessary.

Monthly

- Compare results with predictions and recalculate unit costs if necessary.

- Invoice and collect income.

Quarterly

- Full-scale audit.

- Use comparisons of actuality with forecasts to improve future forecasts.

- Identify any lessons to be learned.

- Research user reaction (i.e., Are charges considered fair? Is the system understood?)

- Are the intended benefits being delivered?

Annually

- Publish reviewed price lists, and cost forecasts.

- Major changes may be necessary. Sometimes deviations from predictions may be due to the introduction of the system itself.

- Decide on any future investment.

It is preferable that charges are stable; otherwise, this will undermine the ability of customers to plan their CAD workload. Thorough monitoring at earlier stages should reduce the likelihood that major changes will become necessary.

Roles and tasks

As with any businesswide system, it is essential that all those involved know exactly what role they are to play.

The Cost Manager

- Supervise and explain the new accounting methods to the rest of the company.
- Analyze the figures and report to the CAD Manager any findings.

The CAD Manager

- Operate the CAD department in a businesslike way, that is, use the figures to ensure efficiency and effectiveness.
- Provide the Cost Manager with relevant data.

The audit team

- View the whole process from a detached position in an overview of the whole proceedings.

Going it alone

The next stage on from being a "Cost Center" is for it to break away completely and become a business in its own right. Larger organizations often find that though there are some advantages to holding on to the CAD/IT department, an isolation from the "real world" can lead to stagnation.

More opportunities exist for revenue generation when freed from the confines of the parent company. For example, outside organizations could be offered bureau services such as CAD drafting and plotting.

What to Do

- Identify costs and the time over which those costs are to be recovered.
- Use this information when setting charges for CAD usage.
- Consider operating as a Cost Center — a strictly cost-managed, financially independent business within a business. This would involve careful planning and implementation, ongoing appraisal, and the allocation of specific roles and tasks in the CAD department.

Glossary

This book treats CAD as an important part of the design industry, not the computer industry, and I hope that this is reflected in the language I have used throughout the book. Unfortunately, the two disciplines do overlap, and designers often find themselves having to interpret the technical jargon written in CAD magazines and spoken by CAD salespeople. The glossary that follows should help with this process by clarifying many of the commonly encountered technical terms.

AEC Architectural, Engineering, Construction. Referring to software applications for the building industry.

B-spline A mathematical technique for joining points together with a smooth curve.

backup A copy of computer files made on different media to be used if the originals are lost or damaged.

benchmark A common set of tests used to compare one computer setup with another.

bill of materials (BOM) An automated calculation of the component parts of a CAD design.

cache A method of computer memory storage that speeds up the transfer of data within the computer.

CAD Computer-aided design. The computerized creation and modification of two- and three-dimensional designs. Applications of this technique are found in all areas of the design industry.

CADD Computer-aided design and drafting. (*See* CAD.)

CAE Computer-aided engineering. The use of computers to solve engineering problems.

CAM Computer-aided manufacture. The programming of computer-operated machinery to perform physical tasks—welding, for example.

CD-ROM Compact disk read-only memory. A portable data storage device with a very large memory that can be read using laser technology.

CIM Computer-integrated manufacturing. The use of computers throughout the whole manufacturing process to coordinate and monitor information as it passes automatically from one function to the next.

crash The unexpected and sudden failure of a computer, often causing work to be irretrievably lost.

data   A general term for the numbers, digits, characters, and symbols stored and processed by the computer.

database   The store of data within the computer.

data processing   The collection, storage, manipulation, and transmission of data.

device driver   A small file on the computer that allows an external device, such as a plotter, to be used by communicating the necessary information to the operating system.

dialog box   An on-screen display area that presents options for the operator to choose from.

digitize   To input information onto the computer by tracing over a paper drawing placed on a tablet with a mouse. (*See* tablet *and* mouse.)

directory   A storage place for files in the computer's memory. Multiple directories and numerous subdirectories may exist.

disk (or disc)   A flat circular data storage device. A *hard disk* is permanently fitted to the computer. A *floppy disk* is portable and can be inserted into a computer, accessed like normal computer memory, and then removed.

display   The visual display unit (VDU) on which the computer image appears.

display list processing   A technique for speeding up the time needed for a drawing to refresh its on-screen image. This is particularly useful for large and complex CAD drawings.

DOS   Disk operating system. The basic software that allows a computer to use other software.

DXF   Drawing exchange format. A text-based computer file that provides a common standard for data transference among many CAD products.

encryption   The conversion of data into a coded form for security reasons.

file   A collection of data, identified by an individual name, held in the computer's memory. Analogous to a file of paper information stored in a filing cabinet.

file server   A computer dedicated to the task of accessing and delivering data to other parts of the computer network (a plotter, for example).

GUI   Graphical user interface. A method of using computers by activating on-screen pictures (icons) that represent commands, applications, and files.

hardware   The equipment that makes up the computer system.

housekeeping   The regular management of the system's memory involving activities such as the removal of unwanted files.

IGES   Initial graphic exchange specification. A standard for the translation of data between CAD systems.

LAN   Local area network. A network of devices within a restricted area.

macro   An automatic routine comprising a batch of commands, often created by the user to simplify a repetitive task.

mass storage A device that will hold vast amounts of data, used to relieve pressure on a computer's memory space.

memory A computer's main data storage facility.

menu The system used for selecting commands in most CAD software. It involves moving the pointing device to a command on the menu and pressing a button to select it.

modem Modulator/demodulator. A device that can convert digital data from a computer into signals that can be transmitted along telephone lines and also reverse the process when receiving a signal.

mouse A pointing device moved by the hand. Its action is translated into movement on the computer screen.

multitasking When more than one program can be run at a time.

multimedia The integration of sound, moving images, and text.

NC Numerical control. The operation of machines by computer programming.

network A common physical link between devices that allows the transfer and sharing of data.

NURBS Nonuniform rational B-spline. An advanced version of the B-spline. (*See* B-spline.)

operating system The collection of programs that supervise the running of other programs on a computer.

pixel Picture element. The smallest visible point on the computer screen. The resolution of an image is indicated by the number of vertical and horizontal pixels.

plot file A CAD drawing "plotted" to an intermediate file which may later be plotted onto paper, even from a computer without CAD software.

plotter An output device that converts CAD data into a paper drawing. Common types are pen, electrostatic, laser, and thermal.

printer A device used mostly to obtain text output, though many can produce graphics also. Common types are: dot-matrix, ink-jet, laser, and thermal.

RAM Random access memory. A memory chip that can have data added to it and read from it directly and rapidly.

raster An image composed of individually lit pixels. The lower the resolution, the more jagged the appearance of smooth curves.

scanning The technique of converting a paper image into digital computer data that can be used in CAD work.

screen The interface between computer and user, used to display text and graphics.

seat An individual CAD installation that may or may not be shared by many users.

software The programs used in a data processing system.

solid modeling   A technique used to build 3-dimensional CAD images out of regular shapes such as spheres and cubes. Boolean expressions can be used to add and subtract these basic shapes to create more complex ones.

surface modeling   A technique used to create smooth 3-dimensional surfaces in CAD work. This would be useful for designing the body of a car, for example, unlike solid modeling.

SVGA   Super video graphics adapter. A graphics standard of high resolution.

tablet   An electronic "drawing board" device, ranging in size from A4 to A0, that senses the motion of the mouse as it moves across its surface. A command menu may be placed on it or a paper drawing, which can then be "digitized" onto the CAD system. (*See* digitize.)

tape   A data storage device that holds CAD data. Analogous to a videotape that holds television signals.

upgrade   An addition or change to a software program to bring it up-to-date.

VDU   Video display unit. (*See* display.)

vector   An image composed of precise mathematically generated lines and curves. A vector image is more suitable to controlling the pen in a plotter than a "raster" image, for example. (*See* raster.)

virus   A type of program that replicates itself and causes havoc within computer systems.

WAN   Wide area network. A network of devices covering a large area, often using public methods of transmission such as the telephone system.

windows   A graphical user interface where, instead of typing commands, icons are selected using a mouse. (*See* GUI.)

wireframe model   A 3-dimensional CAD image made up of lines rather than surfaces, giving it a skeletal appearance.

workstation   A term used to describe the work area of the computer user.

Index

Illustrations are indicated in **boldface**.

ABOUT THE AUTHOR

Ashley J. Hastings is originally from northeast England and has lived in London since 1981. He graduated with an honours degree in Physics from the University of London in 1984.

His scientific background combined with an interest in all aspects of design and led to a career in computer-aided design.

As a CAD Manager and then a freelance CAD Consultant, he has witnessed first-hand the problems facing all areas of the design industry in its attempt to come to terms with the technological revolution.

At present, as a writer and technology consultant, he has a wide brief encompassing magazine articles, industry booklets, television, and books.